CHILDREN'S WELFARE AND THE LAW

The Limits of Legal Intervention

Michael King and Judith Trowell

SAGE Publications
London • Newbury Park • New Delhi

SAGE Publications Ltd
6 Bonhill Street
London EC2A 4PU

SAGE Publications Inc
2455 Teller Road
Newbury Park, California 91320

SAGE Publications India Pvt Ltd
32, M-Block Market
Greater Kailash – I
New Delhi 110 048

British Library Cataloguing in Publication Data

King, Michael
    Children's Welfare and the Law: Limits of
    Legal Intervention
    I. Title   II. Trowell, Judith
    344.204327

ISBN 0–8039–8730–7
ISBN 0–8039–8731–5 (pbk)

Library of Congress catalog card number 92–050384

Typeset by Mayhew Typesetting, Rhayader, Powys
Printed in Great Britain by Biddles Ltd, Guildford, Surrey

Contents

Acknowledgements

We should like to thank the following for their helpful comments on earlier versions of the book:

Martin Richards, University of Cambridge.

Felicity Kaganas, Brunel University Law Department.

Peter Fry, Central Council for Education and Training in Social Work.

Gillian Miles, Tavistock Clinic.

Katherine O'Donovan, Kent University.

We should also like to thank:

Jane Rayner for her excellent typing,

members of the Legal Workshop and other staff from the Child and Family Department of the Tavistock Clinic for their case presentations and valuable insights and

Gillian Stern of Sage Publications for all her help and support.

We are grateful to Brunel University and the Tavistock Clinic for their financial assistance in the research project which formed the basis of Chapter 6, and in the preparation of the manuscript of the book.

1

How the Law Treats Children

Children and the law

It is almost twenty years since the public outcry following Maria
Colwell's death turned child abuse in the United Kingdom into
'legal property'. Before then, the mistreatment of children behind
the closed door of the home was of little interest to lawyers or the
courts. Only if it was so severe that the child died or was seriously
injured or if it took the form of sexual abuse of a gross and scan-
dalous nature would the police intervene and the alleged abuser be
prosecuted in the criminal courts. Now, every day of the week, in
courts all over the country, there are civil proceedings taking place
designed to protect children from abuse, often at the hands of their
parents or step-parents, and to promote their welfare. Specialist
lawyers, specialist judges, specialist police units and specialist
social workers are employed to identify and bring to trial cases
where children have been physically injured by their adult care-
takers or used as sexual objects.

First, the physical abuse of children, then sexual abuse and now
ritualistic abuse – all taking place in the privacy of people's homes
– have been promoted as public scandals with the full glare of
media publicity. The courts have played their part in bringing the
intimate world of adult–child relationships into the public domain.
As ultimate arbiters of truth in our society, they have told us which
children are victims, which adults should be condemned to lose
their children, which should go to gaol.

How the law transforms child welfare

One of the services that the law performs is to transform complex,
messy situations involving intricate human relationships and a
multiplicity of possible causes and effects into a simple story which
makes sense and holds a moral for everyone. The children were
abused. The step-father did it. Or the social workers overreacted.
The children are returned to their homes. Either way, the social
order has been restored. Wicked fathers and step-parents are
punished, while children are placed in good, stable families. Good
parents are rewarded for their perseverance by being reunited with
their children. All is well with the world.

Of course, many of us are parents as well as consumers of
newspaper and television reports of court cases. At one level we all

know that nothing is as simple as these snippets of court judgments seem to suggest. We know also that juries, judges, magistrates, lawyers and social workers are human beings and therefore fallible and yet we accept the findings of the court as 'the truth' of what happened and how it happened, who is to blame, who may be exonerated. To go behind court judgments, to start questioning the wisdom of legal decisions, to start doubting the law's version of the truth would raise serious problems. Not only would it under-mine our confidence that what was done was 'right' for the children in the particular case, but, more crucial still, it would cast doubt upon the very principles that we hold sacred – the right to a full trial of the issues, to one's 'day in court', before being condemned to some formal punishment or to losing one's children. To question the validity of the trial process is to weaken the one protective safeguard that stands between ourselves and arbitrary state power. Without this protection of our basic liberties, our children could be removed from us on the word of an officious social worker. We have a vested interest, therefore, in supporting the law as a truth-finding system and the courts as the final arbiter of what is right and just, even if many of us may have secret doubts.

The price to be paid for legal intervention

Yet in cases involving children's welfare there is a high price to be paid for using the law to protect individual and family rights in this way. The cost is not merely to be measured in financial terms: the price of bringing together highly paid professionals to do combat, using other highly paid professionals to give expert advice to judges and magistrates. The hidden cost, unrecognised by government and by most lawyers, lies in the effects of legal intervention on the children themselves and their relationships with those who care for them. One of the objectives of this book is to explore and expose this uncharted territory.

Most legal cases are fixed in time. They have a clear beginning and end determined by the law's procedures. They start typically with an application for a child protection order – different jurisdic-tions have different names for it – and they end with the making of a final order which sets out who should have legal control of the child, where that child should live and who should have contact with the child. For a few weeks or months all sorts of people are extremely interested in the family's affairs. They open files, inter-view parents and children, carry out detailed investigations, make assessments, ask piercing questions in court and finally provide the world with a judgment. After that, the family ceases to be a legal issue. The judges, magistrates, lawyers and guardians *ad litem* move on to other cases, to other clients. It is often left to those agencies who are not part of the legal machinery to deal with the consequences of litigation for both the children and their past and present care-takers.

Things can go badly wrong
Unfortunately, legal intervention to protect children is no guarantee that the children concerned will be better off at the end of the process than they were at the start. Things can go badly wrong. Let us at this point recount the facts of a recent case just to show how bad that can be.

A young single mother was looking after her three children, aged six, five and three years. Her neighbours complained to the National Society for the Prevention of Cruelty to Children (NSPCC) that abuse was taking place. The NSPCC called in the police after they found that the middle child, a boy, had a black eye, strap marks on his back and a cigarette burn on the back of his right hand. The mother's cohabitee admitted causing the strap mark, but denied that he was responsible for the black eye or the burn. All three children were taken into care under a place of safety order.

Although the children were placed in the same children's home, they were clearly in great distress at being separated from their mother. She visited them regularly. Occasionally her boyfriend would accompany her. The workers at the home noticed that, whenever he came, the boy, who had been abused appeared ill at ease, but the other two children seemed to get on well with him.

The care proceedings were set down for hearing at the local magistrates' court. Since there appeared to be a conflict between the mother's interests in wanting the children home with her and the welfare of the children, a guardian *ad litem* – an independent investigator and adviser – was appointed to represent the children's interests. The guardian then asked for a psychiatrist at the Tavistock Clinic (referred to from now on as 'the Clinic') to carry out an assessment of the children.

The psychiatrist saw the mother, her partner and the three children and was impressed by the mother's parenting capacities and the children's attachment to her. The boyfriend was rather sullen and suspicious, but seemed willing to try to work towards a better relationship with the middle child. The psychiatrist's report to the court ended with a recommendation that all three children should return home, that a care order transferring parental rights to the social services department should be made in respect of the boy, while the other two children should be subject to a supervision order. This conclusion was endorsed by the guardian and by the local authority social worker. Everyone went to court anticipating that there would be no problems.

However, before the hearing took place the mother had moved out of her home in order to get away from harassment by her neighbours, who knew of the abuse allegations. As a result she was adjudged 'voluntarily homeless' by the housing department of the local authority which was not prepared to rehouse her. At the time of the hearing, therefore, she had no home to which the children could return.

In court things went badly. The solicitor handling the mother's case could not attend on that particular day, so a different solicitor was substituted at the last moment. Then, as soon as the local authority solicitor got to his feet, it was apparent that he had not done his homework and did not fully understand the issues before the court. When the magistrates heard about the boy's injuries and the fact that the mother was still seeing the boyfriend, they became highly anxious about the possibility of further abuse. The result was care orders on all three children with the magistrates making it quite clear that they expected the children to remain in local authority care away from their mother.

The consequences for the family were catastrophic. The children were moved to a residential home outside the city. The mother's visits became less and less frequent. Eventually a planning meeting was held to decide the children's future. By this time, for all practical purposes, the family had broken down. Nothing remained but to try to find adoptive parents for the children.

A number of questions spring immediately to mind. Why did it happen? Should the local authority not have offered housing to a mother and her young children? Why employ highly qualified people to evaluate parenting ability and assess where the best interests of children lie, if their advice is then rejected by a bench of magistrates with limited training in these matters? Can it be right that crucial decisions concerning the present and future well-being of young children depend to a large degree upon the quality of the lawyers who appear in court or on the knowledge and understanding of part-time lay magistrates? What purpose was served by legal intervention? Would it not have been much better for everyone concerned if the problem had been dealt with in some other way than bringing in the police, lawyers and magistrates? These too are questions which we shall try to address.

Is law always bad for children?

We do not wish to give the impression at this stage that using the law is always bad for children. It can indeed help to protect them, by, for example, setting down limits for acceptable parental behaviour, by labelling dangerous people and by clarifying the role that different adults should play in the children's lives. It may prod reluctant and overstretched child welfare agencies into action, obliging them to specify the child's needs and offering ways in which those needs may be met. In one case, for example, a boy of two and a half years had been taken into the care of social services along with his brothers and sisters, after the children's mother had developed a psychiatric illness. The child was in a fair physical condition and appeared quiet and contained, often smiling to himself. The social services department's main concern was placing the children, who were of mixed race, with a racially appropriate foster family. When the matter came to court, however, the magistrates took a different view of the children's needs. They ordered a full assessment of each child as an individual with distinctive needs. When this was carried out by the Clinic, it became apparent that the little boy had begun to withdraw into a cut-off autistic-like state. The assessment led to the court specifying a specialist placement for him which offered both permanence and the emotional security and support that he appeared to need.

Unfortunately, such a successful combination of court and clinic working together to secure children's needs is an ideal which is realised only rarely. All too often there are formidable obstacles barring the way to such cooperation, such as the intransigence of parents, the lack of appropriate resources, the irrelevance of many of the legal debates to the promotion of the child's interests. What we have found is that, when the legal system takes over social problems, those things that seemed so important in supporting a family in conflict or suffering hardship and deprivation are often lost from view as minds are concentrated on the pressing legal issues of the evidence, courtroom technique and what strategies to adopt. Of course, despite the impression that Charles Dickens may have given in *Bleak House*, court cases do not go on forever. Sooner or later decisions are made and people are allowed to carry on living their lives. At least the situation will have been clarified; everyone will know where they stand, who has rights and responsibilities in respect of the child and who does not. For the adults concerned this may be a sufficient justification for the trials and tribulations of the legal process. For children, particularly young children, uncertainty and delays, even of short duration, can, as Goldstein et al. have pointed out in their celebrated book, *Beyond the Best Interests of the Child*, cause misery, insecurity and untold suffering.

The paradox of using the courts for child welfare

Yet, in child protection cases and parental disputes over children, delays and uncertainty are the very hallmarks of the legal process. Indeed, the more the law tries to make itself responsive to children's needs and the more the courts transform themselves into tribunals of inquiry into the best interests of children, the longer the delays and the deeper the uncertainties are likely to be. This is a paradox which was largely unrecognised by Goldstein and his co-authors in *Beyond the Best Interests of the Child*. When courts are simply concerned with deciding issues of 'proved' or 'not proved', as in criminal trials, the law can rely upon the 'good sense' of judges, magistrates and juries. But when it is a matter of determining questions about a child's future welfare, this necessarily involves lengthy investigations of the family, the personalities and motivations of the parents, their capacity to care for and protect their child and the child's needs and problems and how the needs can be met and the problems tackled. All this takes time – a considerable amount of time.

The more the legal system takes on itself the burden of protecting children and promoting their interests, therefore, the less able it is to act swiftly to resolve conflicts and provide certainty. If courts were actually able to offer an environment for long-term problem-solving and resources to help children and families in difficulties, there would be less of a problem. Unfortunately, in Anglo-Saxon countries which operate upon an adversarial system of justice this is not possible. Courts are there to make decisions on specific, isolated issues. Furthermore, despite all the trappings of welfarism – the specialist lawyers, the social workers, the mental health experts and the guardians *ad litem* – when it comes to the crucial decision-making, the courts often revert to type and concentrate on issues of 'proved' and 'not proved'. As we shall see from some of the cases discussed, complex issues concerning disturbed and damaged children may, once they enter the legal arena, so easily be transformed into the simple question of whether the abuse did or did not take place. And the outcome for the child depends much more upon the answer to that question than upon a careful analysis of that child's needs.

The law's colonisation

Another unwelcome development is the way in which the law's attempt to turn itself into an institution for determining child welfare issues results in child welfare issues being transformed into law-like issues. It is disturbing when social workers seem more anxious to learn about court procedures, legal strategies, rules of evidence and how to give a good performance in court than about child development and the most effective ways of helping families. It is worrying when codes of conduct which originated as guidelines are treated by courts (and then by the social workers themselves) as strict rules to be followed to the letter and breaches of the code condemned as if they were criminal offences. It is even more worrying when the only way to obtain some scarce resources, such as residential places in specialist schools or mother and child units, is by going to court and persuading the judge to recommend such provision. At a time when politicians on both sides of the Atlantic have been talking enthusiastically about 'rolling back the state', it is not perhaps surprising that social workers from both statutory and voluntary agencies find themselves spending less time working to support and advise parents, and offering services and resources to help needy children, and more time investigating allegations of child abuse, collecting evidence and helping to bring cases before the courts.

The English system of child care and protection

In order for readers to make sense of the case studies presented, they will need to know something about the workings of the system of child care and protection operating in England and Wales. In this section, therefore, we set out what we consider to be those aspects of the system which affect the relationship between court and mental health clinic. The brief account that follows is in no way comprehensive. Readers who require more detailed information should refer to the list of books on the subject set out at the end of this chapter.

At the time of writing, the English law was in the process of undergoing fundamental changes as a result of the introduction of the Children Act 1989. Although the changes brought about by the Children Act were not in force during the period in which our case studies took place, we have where possible tried to indicate the major changes in the legal rules and procedures governed by the Act.

One immediate result of the Act has been the issuing of an abundance of Rules, Regulations and Guidance covering almost every aspect, not only of court proceedings, but also of the roles and duties of public bodies in their care of and relations with children and families. These now have to be consulted and applied whenever a local authority social services department takes any action in relation to a child. Ignorance of their content or failure to comply with them can result in legal action or appeals from legal decisions.

However, while the legal rules and procedures may have changed, the traditions of the English legal system, such as the adversarial nature of court proceedings, the division between solicitors and barristers, the system of appointment of judges and lay magistrates have not. Neither has the organisation and financing of social services departments nor the severe constraints on funds available for them to use in preventive work with families.

Furthermore, we shall be arguing that the basic problems created by the use of the legal process, the creation of codes and guidelines to resolve disputes and to regulate the behaviour of children and parents are not changed by the Children Act and are even likely to be intensified.

Social services departments

The administrative authorities of England and Wales have responsibility for providing such services and amenities as housing, education, public health, planning, road maintenance and social services. General policy and the annual budget for each of the departments providing these services and amenities are decided by elected, unpaid councillors, while the day-to-day running of the departments is in the hands of professional administrators and specialist workers employed by the local authority.

Among the responsibilities of the *social services department* are child care and protection, involving the provision of social work services for children and parents living in the area. These responsibilities range from the running of community homes for children, to the registration and approval of foster families, from the removal of children who are in danger, to the provision of home help for single parents who have problems in coping with child care.

Children may be received *into care* (accommodated) by the local authority on a voluntary or compulsory basis. Where the parents do not request or give their approval for the removal of the child, the social workers are required to obtain a court order before removing the child. Where it is to protect the child from immediate danger, they may obtain a *place of safety order* (an *emergency protection order* under the Children Act 1989) from a magistrate or judge without a full court hearing, but if the removal is to be for more than a few days, they will need to apply to a court for parental rights to be transferred to the local authority under a *care order*. These rights may be restored to the parents only under a further court order, which revokes the care order. The other order that a court may make is a *supervision order*, when the child will usually remain in the home and the parents will retain their rights in regard to the child. Attached to many social services departments is an adoption and fostering agency operated by the local authority. It is responsible for recruiting and approving prospective adoptive parents and for the placement of children with a view to adoption.

The child protection responsibilities of the local authority social workers include the investigation of all allegations of child abuse and neglect. Where these allegations are established, they then have a duty to protect the child, applying, where necessary, for a care order. When the case enters the legal arena, the social workers are assisted by the local authority's legal department, but the responsibility for producing the evidence for the court hearing rests with the social services department and, more specifically, with the social worker or social workers who have been involved with the family.

The police

The main role of the police in relation to children's welfare is in the investigation and prosecution of child abuse cases. In exceptional cases the police can exercise their powers to remove children to a place of safety (see emergency protection, below) and institute care proceedings in the magistrates' court. Recently, the growth of concern over child sexual abuse has seen the police taking on an increasing role in child protection. Police officers now attend case conferences whenever sexual abuse (or serious physical abuse) is suspected and will be present at all initial investigative interviews carried out by social workers.

The magistrates

The magistrates' courts in England and Wales comprise a network of local courts originally with a jurisdiction for criminal cases. This criminal jurisdiction still exists but, in serious cases, such as child sexual abuse prosecutions, it is confined to a preliminary appraisal of the evidence to establish that there is a case to answer. During this century the magistrates' jurisdiction has increasingly extended into civil areas. The magistrates' courts deal with child abuse and neglect cases, adoption and also with matrimonial disputes over custody and access (except where part of divorce proceedings). After the introduction of the Children Act all cases concerning the welfare of children are to be heard by the new *family proceedings court*, which will continue to be situated in the same buildings and the same courtrooms as the previous courts dealing with children's issues.

The overwhelming majority of magistrates are part-time and unpaid, except in the large cities where there are also professional magistrates, whose work tends to be concentrated on criminal cases. It is the *lay magistrates*, unique to England and Wales, who at present determine all child care cases and some disputes over the custody of and access to children. These magistrates are 'ordinary people', from many different walks of life, with no special legal training or knowledge. They are selected for their 'suitability' to do justice, that is to decide cases impartially by weighing the evidence presented to them. After selection there is some basic training in rules of evidence and procedure, court decorum and sentencing powers. A detailed knowledge of the law is not considered necessary, as the magistrates are assisted in court by a clerk who is usually a qualified solicitor or barrister.

Those magistrates who wish to decide cases involving juvenile crime, child care or matrimonial disputes are usually required to sit on the criminal bench for a period and then undertake further basic training to prepare them for their specialist duties. The minimum requirement is for each magistrate to sit for twenty-six half-days per year, although most of them sit far more frequently. The limited time that these non-professional magistrates are able to devote to their duties on the bench precludes any extensive training and results in some unevenness among them in their knowledge and experience of child care issues.

Guardians ad litem
These are people usually with a social work background, but who are not employed by the local authority bringing proceedings. They may be appointed by magistrates' courts (and now by other courts hearing child welfare issues) on a case-by-case basis to investigate the case and make recommendations on what they consider to be the best interests of the child. Originally their appointment was limited to cases where there was a conflict of interests between the child and its parents. However, the Children Act extends their appointment to all cases, unless the court is satisfied that their services are not necessary.

Emergency protection
Orders for the immediate removal of the child could and may still under the new law be obtained from a single magistrate or judge, who does not have to be a member of a specialist juvenile court or family bench. At the time of our case histories these were called

place of safety orders. Under the Children Act 1989 the name changes to *emergency protection orders*. The criteria for granting them becomes narrower and the maximum time that the child could be removed without a court hearing becomes shorter. Usually, there is no formal adversary hearing before the making of a place of safety order, as it is very unlikely that the parents will know that the application is being made and even less likely that they will have found a lawyer to represent them at this stage.

Care proceedings

These can be taken out by the local authority, the police or the National Society for the Prevention of Cruelty to Children. Before any order can be made, even an *interim order*, there has to be a hearing before the magistrates in the juvenile court. For a full *care order* to be made the body applying for the order, usually the local authority, had to prove on the balance of probabilities that one of the grounds under the 1969 Children and Young Persons Act applied and that the child was in need of care and control. Under the Children Act 1989 the court may only make an order where the child is suffering or is likely to suffer *significant harm* or is beyond parental control. At the time of our case histories only the juvenile court magistrates could make care orders. Any applications for revocation of a care order had to go back to the court that made the original order, but not necessarily to the same bench of magistrates.

At care hearings all the parties were and still are likely to be represented by lawyers. In simple, straightforward cases this will involve a lawyer for the local authority, a lawyer for the child and possibly a lawyer for the parents, where the parents' interests do not coincide with those of the child. In more complex cases, as many as four lawyers may be present, including one for each parent. The Children Act is likely to raise this number still further, as grandparents and others who have played a part in the child's upbringing will be entitled to representation in court. In addition to the lawyers, there is also in an increasing number of cases the guardian *ad litem* who may in some circumstances be represented by a lawyer.

Cases proceed according to rules derived from adversarial court procedures, with each party bringing oral evidence in turn for examination and cross-examination. The guardian *ad litem*, where appointed, presents a written report and may be questioned by each party in turn on the contents of that report and its recommendations. Expert evidence from psychiatrists and social workers has to be presented orally, at least until the magistrates have decided that there are grounds for making a *care order* or a supervision order at which point written reports may be submitted.

As can be imagined, care proceedings are often long, drawn-out affairs, sometimes lasting several days. There are occasions when the hearings have to be adjourned for a week or more in order that the same bench of part-time lay magistrates may be constituted. Changes brought about by the Children Act will mean that a written statement setting out the main grounds for the proceedings will be served in advance on the parents. However, where the case is contested, this is unlikely to make the proceedings any shorter or less complicated, as the courtroom testing of oral evidence is still necessary in most instances.

Custody proceedings

This term is used to describe proceedings before any court relating to disputes between parents or parents and others over who shall have the children living with them (contested residence), how frequently and under what conditions the parent who is not awarded custody shall be allowed to see the children (now called 'contact' and previously called 'access') and who shall exercise parental rights in respect of the children (parental responsibility under the 1989 Children Act).

Custody proceedings may take place in several different types of court, depending on the nature of the relationship between the disputants. Where the parents are divorced or are in the process of divorcing, the appropriate court is the County Court, which is presided over by a circuit judge. These are 'generalist' professional judges, appointed to the judiciary by the Lord Chancellor, the government minister responsible for the legal system, from experienced barristers and solicitors. Complex cases may be referred by the County Court to the Family Division of the High Court where the senior judges preside. If the disputants are not divorcing or are not married, custody proceedings usually begin in the domestic (now family proceedings) jurisdiction of the magistrates' courts. As we shall see, wardship judges in the High Court are also able to make orders for custody of and access to children as part of their extensive powers.

At the time of the cases described here there was no power to appoint a guardian *ad litem* in custody proceedings. However, the courts did have various powers to call for reports from social workers and court welfare officers (usually probation officers attached to the High Court or County Court).

Adoption

There are two ways in which children may be adopted in England and Wales. The first is for all the arrangements, including the placement of the child with his or her new parents, to be completed before any application to the court is made. The second procedure allows an adoption agency to apply to the court for the child to be 'freed for adoption' before any placement with prospective parents. Once the child has been living with the adopters for the required period, a further application is made to the court for the transfer of parental rights to be passed to them.

The appointment of a guardian *ad litem* or a social worker to report on the child's situation is obligatory in adoption proceedings. The courts entitled to make 'freeing orders' and adoption orders are the magistrates' court, County Court and High Court. Most cases, however, take place in the County Court. The wardship judge has power to free a child for adoption and make adoption orders.

Until recently, adoption meant the severing of all ties between the child and the original family. Recent judgments, however, have modified this policy, particularly in relation to older children by allowing contact between the child and his or her blood relations, particularly siblings, in exceptional cases.

Wardship

At the time of our case histories anyone who had an interest in a child's welfare could apply to the High Court to have the child made a *ward of court*. If the application was accepted as falling within the court's jurisdiction, the child became subject to wide, paternalistic powers vested in the High Court judge. In addition to its extensive powers to make orders to promote the child's welfare, including care, custody and adoption orders, the wardship court also had a continuing responsibility for the child. It could require periodic reviews of the child's progress. Any major decision, such as a change of school, serious surgery or an alteration in the arrangements for access visits, had to be submitted to the court for approval.

There were, however, restrictions on the use of wardship by parents to challenge the statutory powers of local authorities or the decisions of the magistrates for the removal of a child into care (*A. v. Liverpool County Council* [1982] A.C. 363). These restrictions have been extended by the Children Act 1989 in a way that now prevents wardship being used in any case concerning a local authority. Instead, all applications have to be on the specific grounds for care orders set out in the Act and must be initiated in the magistrates' (family proceedings) court. They may then be dealt with at one of the three levels of courts which operate the family jurisdiction, High Court, County Court or magistrates' court largely according to the complexity of the case.

In wardship the role of representing the child's interests in court, played by the guardian *ad litem* in the lower courts, is undertaken by the *Official Solicitor* or rather by civil servants who work in the Official Solicitor's Department. They will frequently request assessments and expert opinions from mental health clinics. At the hearing they will have instructed a barrister to represent the child's interests.

The wardship jurisdiction is the closest that the English courts come to the kind of continuous judicial supervision found in continental legal systems. Yet in England and Wales the Children Act 1989 places severe restrictions on the use of wardship and in particular over the non-specific powers of wardship courts to deal with any issue concerning a child's welfare.

Child and family mental health clinics

These clinics exist throughout the United Kingdom and are run by a team which usually includes psychiatrists specialising in child and adolescent problems, educational and/or clinical psychologists, social workers, child and adolescent psychotherapists and teachers specialising in learning problems. The team has particular skills in assessing children, adolescents and their families, in communicating with children and in analysing family interaction. It is able to offer opinions on a child's or adolescent's emotional, psychological and social development and on the family's functioning and offer predictions as to future developments.

Clinics also provide training, undertake research and offer a range of therapeutic interventions to relieve distress and to try to improve the functioning of a child, adolescent or family. They may also work with staff in other institutions, such as parent and child units, children's homes, schools, hospital out-patient and in-patient services and social services departments, to assist them in the services that they provide.

Children Act changes

It is not our purpose here to explain or analyse the changes brought about by the English Children Act 1989, particularly as it is far too early to determine the detailed effects of these changes. Readers, however, who are familiar with the Act may wonder whether the problems that we identify were not created entirely by the law as it existed at the time when the cases we describe came to court. Our brief response to the question at this stage is that, while the Children Act may improve the way that the legal system operates in children's cases, it does not tackle the fundamental issue of whether the legal system can deal with the complex and delicate issues raised by child welfare in ways which do not risk harming the child.

The assumption that the Children Act seems to be based upon, at least in the area of public law, is that court proceedings are both appropriate and necessary whenever conflict arises or whenever a statutory body wishes to take any step affecting the parent–child relationship. This is an assumption with which we would wish to take issue. However, we must leave the detailed discussion of this important matter to Chapter 7, by which time we will have presented the main evidence and arguments on which we shall be drawing. At this stage, it would be helpful to bear in mind the major changes of principle *and practice* brought about by the Act which would have been relevant to our cases and which are important to our later discussion of the nature of the legal process.

First of these is the notion of *parental responsibility* which replaces previous concepts of exclusive parental rights and duties. The important point about parental responsibility is that it does not end solely because some other person subsequently acquires it. It can, in other words be shared. This lays the way open for parents to remain responsible for their children even after these children have been removed from the home under a care order in favour of the local authority. Although the local authority has the power to determine in the interests of the child's welfare to what extent a parent shall still be entitled to exercise his or her responsibility, the Act and subsequent Guidelines encourage local authorities to bring parents into a form of partnership and not to denigrate or undermine their responsibility for their own children. Wherever 'practicable' and 'consistent with the child's welfare', placements should be made near the family home. The local authority also has a general duty to 'reunite the child with the family, extended family or other person connected with him'. Parents should be invited to attend review meetings, unless there are 'exceptional circumstances'.

Secondly, there is the express recognition of emotional, intellectual and mental health factors in the statutory definition of 'development', 'abuse' and 'ill-treatment'. Thirdly, is the general principle that whenever a court is considering an order with respect to a child it 'shall not make the order . . . unless it considers that doing so would be better for the child than making no order at all'. This is likely to have important effects in the private law areas of divorce and inter-parental disputes over children, since it allows both parents to retain a responsibility for the child and only where it is in the interests of the child to make an order removing parental responsibility from one of the parents. The needless battles over which of the two parents should have custody and with it all rights and duties in respect of the child, which were provoked by the old law, may now be largely avoided. In the public law area of state intervention for child abuse or neglect, the unwillingness of the court to make an order is likely to be interpreted as a vindication of the party defending the action, whether it be the parents resisting a claim that their child is in need of a care order or the social services department defending the power to retain in place an existing care order.

Fourthly, there is the general principle that in all court proceedings regard is to be had to the harm likely to be caused to a child's welfare by delay in determining issues. Fifthly, the Act introduces a specific requirement that the ascertainable wishes and views of children, appropriate to their age and development should be considered in the decision-making process.

And, finally, there is the consolidation and simplification of laws and procedures concerning children and their welfare, including the standardisation to a large degree of rules of evidence and procedure. While all the changes brought about by the Children Act constitute important reforms of the legal and administrative processes, we shall be arguing in this book that the underlying problems created by the transformation of child care and child welfare concerns into legal issues have not been resolved.

Outline of the book

Our principal objective in this book is to expose to as wide an audience as possible some of the problems encountered when the law seeks to resolve the complex problems of children and their families.

The starting point for our enquiry was a series of Legal Workshops held at the Tavistock Clinic in North West London between 1988 and 1991. These workshops were attended by workers from different professional backgrounds, including child psychiatrists, child psychologists, lawyers, psychiatric and non-specialist social workers and child psychotherapists. At each session one of the participants would present a case in which he or she was involved and which had a legal element. Often the cases presented would concern children and parents who had been referred to the Clinic for assessment by courts or social services departments.

It became apparent as the workshop sessions progressed that there was much anxiety, scepticism and some anger over the way in which many of these cases had been handled in court or over the demands that the courts and social services departments imposed on the Clinic. We identified some themes which drew together some of the problems that people had encountered in legal cases, and we began to move away from individual cases to discussions of courts, the court processes and broader policy issues concerning the use of the law.

Several of the case histories that we discussed during the Legal Workshops are referred to here, along with other cases in which professionals who attended the workshops were involved. However, in order to protect the identity of the Clinic's clients we have not used names, and have slightly altered many of the facts or combined the facts of two or more case histories. These alterations, while important to preserve the anonymity of the children and families, do not change the nature of the issues raised and illustrated by the case(s).

In Chapter 6 we quote from interviews with Clinic workers carried out by Michael King in 1990 as part of a pilot research project to investigate the attitudes of mental health professionals to the courts and legal process in cases involving children's welfare. The results of this study have been published as an article in *The Journal of Social Welfare and Family Law* 1991, although some of the quotations do not appear in the article.

We are aware of the dangers of drawing general conclusions from a limited number of cases from mental health clinics, but we believe, nevertheless, that much of the detailed accounts of what happens to children and families when they become involved in the legal process tends to be lost in confidential files or in the private memories of the individuals concerned. Much of the official research on the issues covered by this book is of a statistical nature and relates to specific social policy issues. It takes little account of the subjective experiences of the individuals concerned or of the effects of legal decisions upon their lives. We therefore offer no apologies for what may be regarded by some readers as the 'unscientific' nature of the evidence presented.

The first part of the title, *Children's Welfare and the Law*, reflects the way in which children's issues are portrayed in much of the literature on child abuse or the effects of the separation of children from parents or a parent. They are seen as existing on the one hand within a system of relations built on feelings of love and caring. Yet, whenever this care system breaks down or has become distorted in ways that are harmful or destructive to the child, law is seen as intervening to impose its rational order, laying down rights, duties and responsibilities, determining what is good or bad for the child. Yet neither caring nor the legal rules on their own can make children thrive or create the environment that children need to sustain them.

In Chapter 2 we examine those social and economic factors that form the background to many of the issues that we shall be discussing. We go on from there (Chapter 3) to look at the different approaches of mental health clinics and courts to the problems presented by child abuse and neglect at the hands of their parents, examining in particular some of the difficulties for such clinics created by the legal process. In Chapter 4 we focus on the specific issue of marital breakdown and its effects on the children who attended the Clinic. We identify some of the problems for the legal process in trying to promote the welfare of children, while at the same time attempting to manage the conflict between the separating or divorcing parents. We then turn to the controversial issue of child sexual abuse (Chapter 5). We describe how clinics have in recent years been used increasingly to provide evidence for the courts and the distorting effect that this has had on the work of the clinic. We voice our concern over the way in which, whenever the spectre of child sexual abuse is raised, all other aspects of that child's needs and welfare seem to vanish from sight as social workers, police, lawyers and judges all seek answers to the two big questions: 'Did it happen?' and 'Who did it?'

In Chapter 6 we present the experiences of expert psychiatric witnesses in court and outside the courtroom drawn from recent research. They describe the ritualistic games that are played during negotiations and court proceedings and both admire and criticise the role of lawyers in the legal process.

The last two chapters pose and attempt to answer some fundamental questions concerning the community's obligations to protect children and meet their needs and what we see as the *limits of legal intervention*. We acknowledge here the importance of protecting individual rights and establishing the facts in the law's operations, but question the wisdom of allowing these objectives to dominate child welfare decisions. We offer our ideal solutions to some of the problem cases that we have described in earlier chapters by putting into practice some of the principles of child care that we believe to be vital if children's needs are to be met by social institutions. In the final chapter we identify what we see as the salient features of a legal system and the ways in which these features may obstruct the promotion of children's interests. We end with a brief examination of how these features have been avoided or their effects mitigated in other systems of conflict management and decision-making processes.

In order to assist readers who wish to follow up some of the issues raised with further reading, we have provided short lists of recent books and articles at the end of each chapter.

Further reading

Law and child psychology, psychiatry and development

Before the Best Interests of the Child by J. Goldstein and A. Solnit (Burnett Books/Deutsch, 1980).

Beyond the Best Interests of the Child by J. Goldstein, A. Freud and A. Solnit (Free Press, 1973).

'Children and the Legal Process: The View from a Mental Health Clinic' by Michael King, *Journal of Social Welfare and Family Law* (1991) no. 4, pp. 269–84.

Children of Social Worlds edited by Martin Richards and Paul Light (Polity Press, 1986).

How the Law Thinks about Children by Michael King and Christine Piper (Gower, 1990).

English family court and child care system

A Guide to the Children Act 1989 by Richard White, Paul Carr and Nigel Lowe (Butterworths, 1990).

The Reform of Child Care Law: A Practical Guide to the Children Act 1989 by John Eekelaar and Robert Dingwall (Routledge, 1990).

The Rights and Wrongs of Children by Michael Freeman (Frances Pinter, 1983).

2

Social and Economic Factors

Much of the published writing on law and child psychiatry/psycho-therapy has tended to focus on the individual and the family unit. We consider it essential to apply a somewhat different approach by setting out from the start what we identify as the important social and economic factors which affect the lives of those children and families who are referred to mental health clinics. It is not our intention here to enter into party political debates over welfare policies, but rather to set the backcloth to the case histories that we shall be presenting and to the legal and therapeutic issues that they raise.

First, a word about the individualising tendencies of law and child psychiatry/psychotherapy. Law in post-industrial countries tends to focus on the nuclear family as a legal unit. The law defines the rights, duties and responsibilities of family members. When things go wrong, it is because rights have not been respected, duties neglected and personal responsibilities ignored or avoided. This does not mean necessarily that the parents or substitute parents who have care of the child are morally at fault, but that it is to them that one looks as having primary responsibility for any harm that might have been caused and to rectify that harm in future.

Child psychiatry and psychotherapy have tended to emphasise the family as the dynamic system which to a large degree determines the mental health or illness of its children. From this perspective, when things go wrong, the problem lies with the relationship that the child has experienced usually with adult members of the family. Individuals within that unit or the family unit itself will often be regarded as pathological with the pathology being passed on to the children. Clinical interventions are aimed at changing the functioning of the family either by working with the whole family unit, for example in family therapy, or with some or all of the family members on their own through child therapy or parent counselling.

Within these individualising discourses the social meaning – all those environmental and circumstantial factors which are outside the immediate control of the family – tends to be lost as a cause of harm to children or as a way of alleviating harm. Here we are referring to such divers factors as lead from car exhausts, poverty, food additives, overcrowding, unemployment and poor nutrition. This does not mean to say that all lawyers and mental health workers as individuals are unaware of these factors, but rather that the professional framework in which they work tends to exclude considering them as appropriate explanations for parents' or children's behaviour. Even where they do admit them as factors in the explanatory discourse, the legal and mental health professionals have very little influence over them, so that what tends to happen is that they become peripheral to the main thrust of courtroom or clinical discussions.

Another criticism of psychiatrists (and to a lesser extent of psychologists) which is frequently voiced by both lawyers and social workers is that one often finds two psychiatrists locked in serious disagreement over the causes of a child's problems and over what should be done to meet that child's needs. In part this stems from a misguided attempt to use psychiatry as if it were an exact science and therefore capable of being used accurately to predict outcomes. In common with other social sciences it is quite possible in psychiatry for several different theoretical interpretations of behaviour to exist alongside one another. These theories are largely constructed for therapeutic or diagnostic purposes and not as a guide to decision-making on child welfare issues. Each may be equally valid on its own terms, but each may emphasise different aspects of the child's being. Whether the predictions of one are likely to be more accurate than those of another cannot be assessed simply by comparing the different theories. Where psychiatrists disagree in practice over what is likely to be best for a child, such arguments are likely to take the form, not of differences in theoretical orientation, but of differences of opinion based on divergences in their experience, knowledge and value-orientation. Admittedly, this can be confusing for lawyers or social workers who wish to see psychiatrists as the source of all wisdom concerning children's welfare, able to provide certainty in an otherwise uncertain world.

However, it is relatively rare in the English courts to find two psychiatrists giving diametrically opposed views as to what the child's needs are and how they may be met. Where this happens it is usually the result of the opposing parties to legal proceedings actively seeking out a psychiatrist who will support their claim. This contrasts with the American system where, first, psychiatrists are much more widely used in court cases and, secondly, are much more willing to give opinions (for a fee) on what is good or bad for a child in any given situation.

The conflicts of opinion that seem for many people to character-ise the state of psychiatry may be seen, therefore, more as a product of the legal process and the demands made of psychiatrists by that process than as emerging from the theories that psychiatrists use. The important point that is often forgotten in relation to child psychiatrists in particular is that these are people who spend most of their working lives with unhappy children and their families trying to understand motivations, causes and effects and attempting to help relieve the unhappiness. Their successes and failures provide them with a wealth of experience about situations of conflict and misery in many different families and about what can be done to help. This experience can be extremely valuable in assisting social workers to cope with continuing problems with difficult families. This is a different use of psychiatrists from that often demanded by courts, where immediate decisions have to be made as to which parent should look after a child or whether a child should be removed from the home.

Some critics of psychotherapy also claim that the concentration upon individual and family pathology systematically deflects attention away from these environmental factors and from the government policies which cause them and allow them to continue. Several feminist writers have also argued that to 'pathologise' women who fail to protect their children against male abusers is to perpetuate and give substance to the patriarchy which, they claim, is the dominant force in modern society. It is not our purpose in this chapter either to support or criticise these claims. What we propose to do rather is to examine the relationship between, on the one hand, social policies and the ideologies that generate them and, on the other hand, the specific problems concerning children and families which are daily confronted by clinic and court.

The Tavistock Clinic's clientele

The Clinic operates as a centre for mental health problems within the National Health Service. The principle under which the whole of the National Health Service in the United Kingdom operates is that health is a social service and should be available free of charge to everyone. Although, as individuals, workers at the Clinic may take on private patients, none of those families attending the Child and Family Department at the Clinic pays fees. These families may be referred to the Clinic from a wide variety of sources. Self-referrals (40–50 per cent) and general medical practitioners (15 per cent) head the list with the local authority social services departments of London boroughs accounting for about 13 per cent. The families referred from these boroughs are predominantly from low-income families. Many are single parent or reconstituted families.

The majority live in low-rent, low-quality, public housing. The parents or step-parents involved with the care of the children are unlikely to be in consistent full-time employment. It is not unusual for the male member of the family to have been unemployed for several years, with little prospect of finding a permanent job. Although most of the parents are literate, the standard of education is generally very low, most having left school at the earliest opportunity without any academic qualifications. An increasing proportion of families referred come from ethnic minority or mixed-race groups with Afro-Caribbean families tending to be over-represented and Asian (both of Indian and Chinese origin) under-represented in relation to their proportion in the local population.

These family characteristics tend also to predominate in those cases referred by the courts where the proceedings were originally initiated by the local authority. These may be either care cases from the magistrates' courts or wardship cases from the High Court. There is a marked contrast, however, in referrals from divorce cases. Here the families are much more likely to be of white, middle-class origins, economically advantaged with much higher levels of education. Some of these come to the Clinic because one of the marital partners has made allegations of child sexual abuse against the other.

Another major category of families who form the clientele of the Child and Family Department involves a parent or parents with a history of serious mental illness. These may be referred from a variety of sources, including school, local authority, general medical practitioner or hospital. There is a fairly broad class and economic spread among the families with serious mental health histories, but the underprivileged sectors of the community tend to be over-represented.

As we have indicated, most of those families who are referred to the Clinic's Child and Family Department come from those sectors of the population which many different studies have identified as suffering from a wide range of social, health and educational problems. This is not particularly surprising, for it is these groups who receive the greatest attention from social work agencies, the police and the courts and it is through these agencies that they tend to be referred to the Clinic.

This correlation between social and economic deprivation and use of the Clinic's services does not necessarily indicate that the socioeconomic factors are a direct cause of such abnormal behaviour as child sexual abuse, or the neglect or rejection of young children, or for that matter of particular types of mental illness or of mental illness in general. Indeed, there is some evidence from the Clinic's records to suggest that all these problems are to be found in families which suffer no economic disadvantages. Children referred for therapy by 'respectable' parents with successful businesses or professional practices have disclosed sexual abuse. Some of the most abject cases on the Clinic's files of emotional neglect concern children from wealthy families.

What distinguishes the poorer from the richer clients is that it is extremely rare for courts, police or social services to be involved with the wealthy families. If police or social services are involved, that involvement is likely to be low-key and almost apologetic. At the slightest hint of some unwelcome intervention, these families are likely to take evasive or defensive measures. Two cases serve to illustrate how this may happen. In the first, a wealthy family, where both mother and step-father were successful entertainers, was urged to contact the Clinic by the head-teacher of the son's private school. The subsequent assessment showed a very depressed, unhappy boy with suicidal tendencies. It also transpired that the step-father strongly resented him, insisting that the boy kept to his room and did not interrupt his life or interfere in any way with the relationship between him and the boy's mother. When the child's unhappiness and the step-father's feelings of resentment were raised in discussion with the mother and step-father, they rejected any further help from the Clinic, despite being told of the risk that their son might attempt suicide. Instead, they arranged for the boy to be sent away to a boarding school.

In the second case, wealthy parents referred their two young children to the Clinic because of the children's temper tantrums. They were worried that the children might have been sexually interfered with. The Clinic discovered that the children had been involved in sexual activity with the *au pair* and her boyfriend. By then the *au pair* and friend had disappeared, and the social services department, therefore, declined to take any action. The parents were alerted to the possible impact of these experiences upon the two children and the Clinic offered to work with the family in order to help the children. This offer was declined. The parents withdrew their children from any further therapy, found a new *au pair* and resumed their busy lives.

In both these cases there was sufficient concern about the behaviour of the children to warrant some therapeutic intervention and a serious danger that the children's problems would worsen if no help was forthcoming. Nevertheless the parents decided, contrary to the professional advice, not to allow their children to receive help. If this had occurred in the disadvantaged families that are the usual clients of social services departments, it is likely that, at the very least, the children would have been placed on the social services' child protection register and pressure would have been brought to bear on the parents to allow their children to receive help. As it was, both cases had to be abandoned, after repeated attempts to engage the family had failed.

Where attempts have been made to intervene to help children who have suffered abuse within well-to-do families, these have often been met by fierce resistance. There are letters on the Clinic's files from solicitors threatening dire consequences if a member of the Clinic staff should so much as mention their client's name in discussions with other agencies. Other letters insist that the family's lawyer should be present at any meeting of professionals to discuss allegations of child abuse. Many families, therefore, tend to use mental health clinics as a resource to 'cure' their children's illnesses and solve their behaviour problems, but as soon as their own role as parents is questioned, they withdraw from the clinic and use their money to buy solutions for their children which do not cast doubt on their parenting. It is the families who do not have the money or resources to provide private services for their children who tend to find themselves defending their parental rights in court or in case conferences called by social services.

Ideology, policy and resources

One cannot assume a direct relationship between social and economic deprivation and the ill-treatment of children. Clearly, most poor families do not abuse their children, while children from well-to-do homes are not immune from suffering caused by negligent or inappropriate parenting. This does not mean, however, that poverty and social disadvantage have no effect on people's behaviour towards their children. The stresses on family life caused by such social factors as poverty, long-term unemployment or living in overcrowded conditions are well documented. For example, people who experience continuous debilitating stress may use drugs and/or alcohol to escape from the harsh realities of their lives, and drug and alcohol addiction are common factors associated with the physical abuse and neglect of children. Indeed, Valium, the drug that many doctors prescribe for anxiety, is known to have a disinhibiting effect on aggressive behaviour. Then again, the stresses caused by economic disadvantage may also trigger bouts of depression and irrational behaviour among adults who are particularly vulnerable to mental disorders of this kind.

The separation or divorce of parents now affects almost one in three children on the Clinic's files. Although children from all social classes and ethnic groups are affected, the impact is likely to be much less catastrophic for the child where the family has the financial resources to cope with the splitting of the household and/or the support of an extended family to cope with the emotional impact. A high proportion of the cases referred to clinics from courts and social services departments has neither of these assets. Many of the children have a history of family instability, never knowing their fathers or experiencing family breakdown at an early age. In referrals relating to sexual or physical abuse, the alleged abuser is frequently a cohabitee or a boyfriend of the child's mother and less often the child's natural father.

The problems referred to clinics cannot neatly be classified as mental health issues to be treated and cured by deploying the clinical staff's therapeutic skills. The original conception of the Tavistock Clinic as offering a specialist service to children and families within the free-health-for-all policy of the welfare state pioneers of the 1940s was seriously flawed. This ideal failed to appreciate the relationship between mental health and social disadvantage and deprivation. Unfortunately, no amount of counselling and psychotherapy is likely to make much impact on families suffering from multiple problems associated with poverty. One can hardly expect children whose lives are insecure and unstable, who lack the basic amenities for fulfilling their needs as emergent human social beings, such as proper nutrition, a solid physical environment which they can call 'home' and education and play opportunities to provide adequate intellectual stimulation, to blossom forth into normal development after a programme of visits to the psychotherapist for an hour a week.

The problems that constantly stare clinical workers in the face arise not so much from the subtleties of transference and counter-transference as from the struggle to secure resources to meet children's fundamental needs. These problems have increased markedly in recent years with the arrival of government policies of promoting individualism, cutting public spending and giving a free rein to market forces.

However, it would be wrong to suggest that these resource problems began with the rise of individualism and the right-wing policies of the eighties. Any policies which leave certain social groups vulnerable to stress, ill-health or discrimination are potentially damaging to children's welfare. The hardline taken by governments in Britain and the USA has had the effect of removing the safety nets that these groups relied upon to prevent a bad situation turning into one of helplessness and despondency.

Ironically, general policies designed to strengthen the family and promote children's interests may have serious adverse effects for some of the more vulnerable children and their parents. Examples of such policies abound in the legislation passed by the Conservative government in the United Kingdom in the mid-eighties to encourage parents to accept their responsibilities. Perhaps the most notorious (later admitted as a mistake by the government) withdrew accommodation allowances for teenagers who left home, which had the effect of leaving many young people 'living rough' on the streets of London and other major cities.

Even well-intentioned policies, based on sound theoretical ideas concerning children's needs, when put into practice in an inflexible, dogmatic manner, are likely to prove damaging to some categories of children. A powerful ideology which swept through English social services departments in the late seventies held that all children prospered best in a family environment. This ideology combined with a period of financial stringency led to the closing down of several hundreds of children's homes throughout the country. Admittedly, many of these homes were expensive and inefficient and their staff underqualified and poorly paid. Nevertheless, this was hardly a justification for the strategy adopted by at least one county council of closing down every one of its residential homes and sticking, in the face of severe criticism, to a policy of trying to find foster families for all children, regardless of age and background, because 'it seems right for children'.

Yet, while this de-institutionalisation policy may have served the needs of the majority of children, it took no account of evidence that there exist certain categories of children who have great difficulty in adapting to 'new families'. These include highly disturbed children who find the emotional intensity of family life too much to bear, and adolescent children who rebel against the constraints of a family setting. Yet when this policy was translated into social action, it became virtually impossible to find residential places for these children. Fostering and more fostering was the order of the day.

Sometimes it worked and children made enormous progress in their newly found homes. In far too many cases, however, the fostering placement broke down with the result that the children experienced yet another failure in their short lives and another rejection. Studies of fostering showed that large numbers of children suffered at least one fostering breakdown and some experienced as many as five or six. These failures and rejections took place at a time in these children's lives when they needed stability above all else.

The 'fostering revolution' had major repercussions for the legal process. Many long-term foster parents understandably grew attached to their young charges and not unnaturally wished to see their relationship with the child secured through adoption. At a time when there were far too few normal, white European babies to meet the needs of all those couples wishing to adopt, the long-term fostering of children who had been removed from their natural families became a legitimate alternative way of obtaining such children. The courts started to see an increasing number of applications for 'forced adoptions' – that is, adoption of children whose parents had not consented. These usually concerned children who had been removed from their natural families some two or three years previously following a finding in the courts of child abuse or neglect. Social services departments developed policies of cutting off contact between children and their natural families in order to prepare the children for adoption and in anticipation of the court application. This in turn led to the emergence of pressure groups such as the Family Rights Group to assist parents in the fight to keep their children.

We offer this account of how forced adoptions became accepted as the best way of securing the welfare of seriously abused and neglected children not so much as a criticism of social services departments and the social workers who staffed them but as an illustration of the relationships between political ideology or dogma, social policy and the legal process. This interweaving of dogma, economic constraints and bureaucratic rigidity also had direct effects on the work of the Clinic. It provided the framework within which questions were formulated by social services departments and the courts and which Clinic 'experts' were expected to answer – preferably simply and without reservations. The issue was (and, on occasions, still is) presented as a stark choice between the natural family which has failed or abused the child and the prospective adoptive family with whom the child is now living. In most of these cases it hardly needs to be stated that the natural family suffers the sorts of social disadvantages described earlier, while the prospective adopters have many of the attributes that one associates with an ideal family.

For hard-pressed social services departments, adoption has the distinct advantage over fostering or supporting the natural family, in that, once achieved, the child is no longer their responsibility and ceases to be a burden on public funds. What appears at first sight as a relatively simple case of trying to find the best solution for the child, reveals a history of policy choices which have led to the present situation and the seeming inevitability and desirability of the adoption going ahead.

One case that illustrates this point concerns a young couple with housing and financial problems. They had two young children with sleeping difficulties. The sleepless nights and the stress of coping with the children within a confined living space led to fights between the parents. Social services were alerted when the elder child, aged four, was found with bruises. Despite social work support and nursery placements for the children, the fights continued. The younger child, then twenty months old, suffered a fracture to the upper arm and the children were both removed and placed in foster care under a care order.

The months passed and still the parents continued in the same pattern. Each blamed the other for the loss of the children and there was little prospect that they would be able to provide a secure home for their children. The father began to drink, while the mother became depressed. Their visits to the children became more and more infrequent and erratic. After two years, social services decided to free the children for adoption with the idea that the foster parents would eventually be the adopters. The mother, who had recovered from her depression, contested the case, but was unable to convince the judge that she would be able to provide a stable home for the children. In the circumstances adoption was probably the best solution for the children, but if better housing and more intensive help for the couple to overcome their relational problems and sustain contacts with the children had been available, there could have been a very different outcome.

Although the 'fostering revolution' now appears to have run its course and the pendulum in the United Kingdom, with the passing of the Children Act 1989, seems to be swinging back in favour of the natural family, the tendency for policies to be ideologically driven rather than determined by the needs of individual children remains unchanged. The recent controversy over trans-racial fostering is a powerful example of this process. Certain local authorities have imposed a strict policy of not placing black children with white or mixed-race families, because of a belief that a child's racial identity takes precedence over all other considerations. What concerns us is that where this policy is applied indiscriminately with little regard for the child's individual needs, it is clinics and the courts that are left to pick up the pieces and try to patch up what has by then become a desperate situation for the child.

Scarce resources and the courts

The 'Thatcher years' between 1979 and 1990 were difficult times for mental health clinics and for many of those children and families who made use of the services of such clinics. First, there were the obvious effects that one would expect when a government virtually turns its back on the welfare state by making a virtue of cuts in public spending. Social security provision and those public services, such as health and education, which had no income independent of government funding, underwent a traumatic reduction and deterioration. Despite government claims that it was targeting resources at those with the greatest need, it was inevitable that the poorest, most socially disadvantaged individuals and families were the ones which took the main brunt of these cuts. Changes in social security rules, as we have seen, drastically cut any payments to unemployed young people, in order, so it was said, to reinforce family responsibility. One result was a drift of teenagers to London and other large cities, where many would end up sleeping in shop doorways and begging in the streets.

Cuts in local authority social services meant that in those London boroughs with major social problems, only the most urgent cases were accepted. In some instances several months would elapse after the report of abuse or neglect before a social worker would be assigned to the case. In one London borough the social services department simply refused to take on any new cases. The rapid turnover of social workers in these hard-pressed boroughs made any consistent monitoring of children's progress extremely difficult. Often clinics which had been treating the child knew more about the family and its problems than the social workers involved. Increasingly, those social workers who remained in the public sector were pushed into the role of social police – a reactive force which moved into action whenever such serious abuse had taken place that not to have taken action would have resulted in the public pillorying of social workers in the media. The preventive work which had been developed in the sixties and seventies simply fell by the wayside. There were no funds to keep it going. For a management obsessed with cost-efficiency, the benefits were too vague and too long-term to warrant funding. In any event, it was not acceptable to central government, which saw many of the preventive schemes as perpetuating people's state of dependency by removing from families the necessity to take responsibility for their own members.

At the Tavistock Clinic, in particular, more and more of the work seemed to take the form of acting as a catalyst, trying to persuade social services departments to help families and protect children at risk. Where the persuasive powers of clinical reports failed to have any effect, the only recourse left was to put the matter before the courts in the hope that a sympathetic judge would use his or her authority to force some action from the local or central government department. Sometimes this worked well. In one case two children, a boy aged nine and a girl aged eleven, were surviving with great difficulty on the battlefield created by their warring parents. As matters became progressively worse between the parents the harm to the children was increasingly apparent. The best solution to the problem seemed to be a co-educational boarding school which would allow the children to remain together. The local education authority's reaction to this proposal was to state that there were no places available in state boarding schools and no funding for private schools. The children were made wards of court. When the judge read in the court reports of the response of the education authority he summoned the local education manager to appear before him and virtually ordered him to find a solution. Very soon after the manager was able to tell the court that adequate funds had been found to pay for private schooling.

In another wardship case where three children had been sexually abused by a previous partner of their mother, the family needed transport to take them to the Clinic for weekly treatment sessions. Neither social services nor social security was prepared to pay the cost. When this was reported to the judge he ordered the local authority social services to make the necessary transport arrangements for the family to receive the treatment that the court had approved.

Victories for common sense, for children's welfare, over penny-pinching bureaucracy perhaps. If one pauses to reflect on such seeming victories, however, a number of difficult issues emerge. For a start, the fight was necessary in the first place only because central and local government had not allocated sufficient resources to meet the needs of children in trouble. Adequately resourced, efficiently managed education and social services departments would not have rejected perfectly reasonable requests for children's needs to be met. Secondly, leaving it to individual judges to take the initiative seems a strange way to allocate resources. What happened to the many children in a similar position to those in the two case histories who did not become the subject of court proceedings or whose case came before a judge who was not prepared to tell government departments how they should spend their money? Thirdly, given the delays, expense, anxiety and acrimony associated with adversarial legal proceedings, are courts really the best place to resolve such issues? These are matters which we shall take up again when we come to discuss the social functions of the law in Chapter 7.

Summing up

1. The concentration by courts and clinics on individual children and individual parents excludes from consideration and from the decision-making ·process a wide range of social factors which affects families and the way that children are treated within them.

2. Almost all the Clinic's clients who are referred by social services departments or courts in child care and wardship cases come from low-income families living in conditions of social deprivation. This contrasts markedly with court referrals from matrimonial disputes where the families tend to be predominantly middle class, living in conditions of financial security and relative comfort.

3. Where families suffer from a multitude of social and economic disadvantages and deprivations it is hardly surprising that parent–child relationships become strained and that stress factors, or drugs or alcohol used to escape from stress and unhappiness, play their part in the incidence of child abuse. Where children lack the basic amenities for fulfilling their physical and social needs, there is little that treatment at a child mental health clinic can do to improve their lives.

4. Parents from professional and other socially advantaged backgrounds will often use the services provided by mental health clinics to help them cope with children who are seen as having psychological or learning problems. However, as soon as there is any hint of official concern about the possibility of abuse or the quality of parenting, they tend to remove the children from therapy and, in extreme cases, send them off to private schools or move the family out of the area.

5. Right-wing, anti-interventionist policies, together with major cuts in public spending, have drastically reduced both the range and the quality of services available to help disadvantaged families. This has had a marked impact on the support available for families whose children attend clinics. It has also meant that clinic workers find themselves trying to liaise with agencies where staff are overworked and constantly changing and which can offer only limited child protection services.

6. Government policies have also affected legal decisions in child care and wardship cases in that these have to be taken in the context of available resources for family support and substitute

care. The lack of sufficient places in children's homes and the scarce facilities for nursery education are two examples. The rise in 'forced' adoptions and the 'family rights' reaction to them can be seen in part as resulting from a failure to provide adequate substitute care and child support facilities for poor families.

7. In some cases the authority of judges has been used to obtain scarce resources for children which would not otherwise have been made available. While this may have improved the situation of individual children, there are strong reservations of principle in using the courts in this way.

Further reading

The effects of deprivation upon families

Automatic Poverty by William Jordan (Routledge, 1981).

'Family Relationships, Life Events and Childhood Psychotherapy' by Ian Goodyer, *Journal of Child Psychology and Psychiatry* (1990) 31, no. 1, pp. 161–92.

Inequalities in Health by Peter Townsend and Nick Davidson (Penguin, 1982).

Poverty, Explanations of Social Deprivation by Robert Holman (Martin Robertson, 1978).

Public Issues and Private Pain: Poverty, Social Work and Social Policy by S. Becker and S. McPherson (Insight Books, 1988).

Putting Families First by Robert Holman (Macmillan, 1988).

'Vulnerability to Childhood Problems and Family Social Background' by D. M. Fergusson, L. J. Horwood and J. M. Lawton, *Journal of Child Psychology and Psychiatry* (1990) 31, no. 7, pp. 1145–60.

Thatcherism and its effects

Punishing the Poor: Poverty under Thatcher by K. Andrews and J. Jacobs (Macmillan, 1990).

Thatcherism edited by Robert Skidelsky (Chatto and Windus, 1988).

Thatcherism, a Tale of Two Nations by Bob Jessop and others (Polity Press, 1988).

The Thatcher Decade: How Britain has Changed during the 1980s by Peter Riddell (Basil Blackwell, 1989).

Substitute care: fostering, adoption and children's homes

Adoption: Essays in Social Policy, Law and Sociology edited by Philip Bean (Tavistock, 1984).

Black Children in Care: Evidence to House of Commons, Social Services Committee by the Association of Black Social Workers and Allied Professions (HMSO, 1983).

Children who Wait: A Study of Children needing Substitute Families by Jane Rowe and Lydia Lambeth (The Association of British Adoption Agencies, 1973).

Foster Home Breakdowns by D. Berridge and H. Cleaver (Blackwell, 1987).

'Intercountry Adoption: A Review of the Evidence' by B. Tizard, *Fostering and Adoption* (1991) 32, no. 5, pp. 743–56.

'Intercountry Adoption: In Whose Best Interests?' by Damien Ngabouziza, *Fostering and Adoption* (1988) 12, no. 1, pp. 35–40.

Lost in Care: The Problems of Maintaining Links between Children in Care and their Families by Spencer Millham and others from the Dartington Social Research Unit (Gower, 1988).

The Placement Needs of Black Children, practice note 13 (British Association of Adoption and Fostering, 1989).

Recollections and Disruptions by J. Aldgate and D. Hawley (NFCA, 1986).

Physical abuse

Child Abuse: Professional Practice and Public Policy edited by Olive Stevenson (Harvester Wheatsheaf, 1989).

The Common Secret by Ruth Kempe and Henry Kempe (W.H. Freeman, 1984).

The Darker Side of Child Abuse edited by D. J. Finkelhor, Richard J. Gelles, Gerald T. Hotaling and Murray A. Straus (Sage, 1983).

'The Jasmine Beckford Affair' by Robert Dingwall, *Modern Law Review* (1986) 49, no. 4, pp. 489–507.

The Role of Violence in Child Rearing by Alice Miller (Virago, 1983).

See also official child abuse inquiries in Further Reading Chapter 3.

Effects of separation and divorce

Mate and Stalemate: Working with Marital Problems in a Social Services Department by J. Mattinson and I. Sinclair (Basil Blackwell, 1979).

See also Further Reading in Chapter 4.

3

Court and Clinic: Different Perceptions of Parenthood

The problems described in this chapter concern the different ways in which clinics and courts perceive and deal with child–family situations. While the cases described occurred in English courts, the problems that they reveal are in no way a product uniquely of the English legal system. Indeed, problems arising from such differences are just as likely to occur in the continental inquisitorial system as in the Anglo-American adversarial system. Whether it is either realistic or desirable to try to reduce these differences of perception, understanding and decision-making through training or to act as if they did not exist, by promoting the overriding objective of the child's welfare, are matters which we shall take up in Chapters 7 and 8. What this chapter seeks to show is how difficult it is at times for those who work in mental health clinics, on the one hand, and the judges, magistrates and lawyers who function in court, on the other, to relate to one another on child welfare issues. These difficulties are not a product of personal preferences or animosities, but they arise, rather, because each social institution has its own way of classifying and conceptualising issues.

Much of the official rhetoric of child abuse inquiry reports in Great Britain gives the impression that the answer to every problem lies in inter-professional communication and cooperation. When things go wrong, as they often do, the blame is laid at the door of inefficient individuals, ineffective systems and poor communications. This conveys that somewhere, somehow there can exist an ideal system which we should all be aiming for – a system where children will be protected, parental rights respected and lawyers and child care 'experts' will work in perfect harmony. What we argue in this chapter is that this vision is quite unrealistic, for the so-called failures of communication are, in our view, symptomatic of fundamental differences in professional orientation which cannot be reconciled.

These differences cannot be described as philosophical, since they do not necessarily arise from any deeply held convictions about children's welfare or the role of parents. Nor are they politically inspired, for often clinical staff and lawyers will support the same political party and share common views about government policies towards children and families. The most appropriate word to describe them is *institutional*, for they are a product of the institutional differences between law and a medical/scientific approach, which in turn arise from the different social functions of institutions such as courts and clinics.

In this chapter we take a variety of issues concerning parents and children and show the extent of the differences between clinic and court in the ways in which these situations are perceived, classified, discussed and disposed of either as a 'problem solved' or for further work by other institutions.

Confidentiality

One of the major influences of the courts on the Tavistock Clinic's day-to-day work concerns the keeping of records. This influence has had both good and bad effects on the practice of mental health professionals and their relationships with patients. In the past they were in the habit of keeping records of consultations, interviews and therapy sessions haphazardly in their own style. The files would contain observations, findings and test results all jumbled up together. There was never much thought given to the repercussions or implications of this practice.

The increased involvement in court work has changed all this. For many at the Clinic this involved a difficult period of learning. They had to learn how to keep records in ways that allowed them to extract relevant information to support with firm evidence the opinions and conclusions set out in their reports to the courts. When the first requests for reports started to come from the courts, there was considerable confusion and anxiety among many of the professionals concerned. Some even went so far as to refuse to write reports for legal cases because they felt that to do so would be breaching the client's confidentiality. When reports were produced, they tended to be short and bland. Only gradually did they become more detailed and set out the views of the mental health professional in ways that were of use to the court.

However, the demands from the legal system did not stop with requests for reports. With the increase in prosecutions and child care proceedings for sexual abuse came lawyers asking to inspect the Clinic's files and subpoenas ordering the files to be handed over to a judge. Nor was it only the patients' files that were required. Video tapes that had been prepared for therapeutic or training purposes were transformed into 'evidence' to support the view that abuse had or had not occurred. There were the inevitable conflicts over the Clinic's concern to protect from the public gaze patients' health records and the right of defendants accused of serious crimes to evidence which might prove their innocence. In civil cases the files or video evidence might give valuable support to the social services department bringing child protection proceedings or the parents defending the right to keep their children.

It has always been the policy of the Clinic to allow individual patients to know of information about them kept in clinical files. Under the Access to Health Records Act 1990 patients are now entitled by law to this information. In some cases this information may be helpful to the patient as evidence in court proceedings. However, major problems arise if there is information in the health records about people other than the patient in criminal activities such as child sexual abuse. These problems increase where the patient is a child and the defendant in criminal proceedings the parent of that child. Should the information be handed over to a defendant's solicitor? What should a psychiatrist do when he or she is asked to bring the medical records to court and to be prepared for cross-examination on their contents?

These conflicts of interest, we should emphasise, did not occur when the Clinic specifically agreed to undertake legal work. Here there was no question of confidentiality. The interviews and video recordings were undertaken with the clear objective of providing a report for the court. This use of clinics as an extension of the legal system may lead to other problems, as we shall discuss later, but the question of privacy or confidentiality of records did not arise here. The most serious difficulties occurred rather in those cases where individual or family therapy had taken place some time before there was any hint of court proceedings. Therapists frequently held tapes or notes of sessions where the patient's private world was discussed and fantasies explored – all on the basis that what occurred in therapy was confidential between therapist and patient. Some months or years later, there was a criminal prosecution, or care or wardship proceedings, where the records or tapes were seen as important items of evidence.

In recent years various compromise arrangements have emerged which go some way towards resolving the conflict between the principle of confidentiality and the right to present in court all relevant evidence in the interests of justice. Tapes made as a record of clinical (as opposed to legal) interviews are not released, unless the judge so orders. Lawyers are given permission by the Clinic to come to the Clinic and view the tape, but no copies are released, unless the court so orders.

Adult patients have a right to expect confidentiality in regard to any records concerning their health. Under the Access to Health Records Act, they also have a right of access to their own records.

Unless the court makes a specific order concerning these confidential records, nobody else is permitted to see them. If the patient is under eighteen, the right of access to records will depend upon the age and maturity of the young person. The only exception to the confidentiality principle concerns the disclosure of records in order to protect children from abuse. Where during an interview or course of therapy an adult patient discloses that he has abused his child, the clinical worker is obliged to inform social services. A similar principle applies if a child discloses that they have been the victim of abuse.

Where the court subpoenas a clinical file, it may be made available at the Clinic to the lawyers involved, who may take notes, but not copies. Where the file contains particularly sensitive material, for example, concerning people not directly involved in the proceedings, it may be sent to the judge who will read the file and decide whether it should be released to the parties or whether all or part of the file should remain confidential. Where the file is released, it is possible for press and public to be excluded from court whenever there is cross-examination on matters concerning people who are not parties to the proceedings.

Despite these arrangements, there are still difficulties for therapeutic relationships. Previously, the cast-iron assurance of confidentiality that clinics were able to offer encouraged patients to reveal aspects of themselves and their lives which could be of considerable value in the therapeutic process. The increased legal involvement has created an awareness by some patients that what they say in therapy sessions may not be treated with total confidence. This on occasions has led to suspicion and lack of trust detracting from the quality of the relationship between therapist and patient.

If, during the course of therapy, a court asks for a clinical report, the nature of this relationship is likely to change completely. The report has to be prepared and then discussed with the patient or patients involved. Parents may, for example, demand an explanation of information contained in a court report or of the recommendation it contains. Frequently, they find aspects of the report upsetting and disagree with its conclusions. On occasions the views expressed in the report may be so unacceptable to the parents that it becomes impossible to undertake any future work with the family.

For the Child and Family Department, the principal patient is the child and not the family. It is the child's best interests which are always the paramount consideration. However, it is often difficult to separate as a unit of interest a child from its family and

its parents, so that this principle of the child's interests as paramount is not as helpful as might appear. As we shall see in some
of the case histories which appear in later chapters, this change in
the Clinic's role from therapeutic to legal work risks not only
alienating the parents, but also may jeopardise any possibility of
future work with the child and family.

Individual work with children

It is usual working practice when conducting therapy sessions with
a child for the therapist to record the dialogue in some detail.
These notes will record discussions about actual events and
experiences in the child's life as well as fantasised events existing
only in the child's internal world. By making links between the
external and the internal, the therapist will attempt to help children
unravel and make sense of their experiences and their behaviour.
The note-taking process enables therapists to retain their objectivity and trace themes and conflicts as they emerge from the
therapeutic dialogue. These notes make no distinction between
fantasy or reality, fact or opinion. Everything is taken down for
later reflection and analysis.

When a child in therapy tentatively begins to disclose abuse, the
notes will record all references to these disclosures. These notes
are, however, not part of the patient's file. They represent rather
the raw material on which the therapist then works and, as such,
may contain much fantasy, associations and vague intimations.

At the point when the therapist begins to recognise the abuse as
reality rather than fantasy, then this recognition is shared with the
child and the therapist explains that the confidentiality of the
sessions must be broken and information passed on to those
colleagues at the Clinic with management responsibility. On a
number of occasions at the Tavistock Clinic, these 'process-record'
notes, which were not part of the formal clinical file, have been
subpoenaed by a judge and used in court. Much of the material
was totally irrelevant to the case and its disclosure caused distress
to the children and their carers.

The issue as to who 'owns' the notes and who should have a
right to see them remains confused. The clinical record is where
therapists set out their understanding of the child's difficulties,
behaviour and relationships, and record any progress made by the
child. To expose to the scrutiny of strangers the therapist's process-
record notes seems to us and to most therapists an invasion of the
child's private space where he or she may explore experiences and
feelings with safety and confidence. The situation is aggravated
further when these notes are subpoenaed where an ambiguous

suggestion of sexual abuse has been made by the child and attempts are made in court to ascribe meaning to the confusion of fact and fantasy that has emerged from the therapy sessions.

Video tapes and family therapy files

In family therapy all the information about family members is kept in a 'family file'. Video recordings, where they are used, show family members discussing issues among themselves. Both the files and the tapes may contain information and views expressed about other members of the immediate family, extended family, former partners, step-children, etc. who were not present at the sessions. On occasions the people mentioned may be interviewed to provide reality-testing information for the therapists.

Child abuse may emerge as an issue either during family therapy or after the therapy has been completed. In one case the allegations arose some three years after the end of the therapy. Tapes may be subpoenaed and all of a sudden work that was conducted on the basis of confidentiality is exposed to all parties to the proceedings. Opinions, beliefs and information which have no bearing on the case are revealed for all in court to see. Trust is undermined.

Record keeping

There is a worrying effect on professional practice arising from the concern among clinical workers that they may be ordered to produce their files in court or make copies of notes of interviews and observations of behaviour available to lawyers. Increasingly, these professionals appear to be writing less and less in the files, and are becoming very circumspect about what they record in writing. Facts can be written down, but impressions, opinions and hypotheses are omitted. The only record of them is kept in the heads of the professional concerned. Yet in the clinical setting we know that it is only as the opinions and impressions of different professionals come together and are confirmed by other agencies that it is possible to build up a picture of possible abuse.

While it may be important that professionals do not make judgements based on their own prejudices and unjustified assumptions (particularly those associated with race, culture, gender and sexual orientation), there is in the area of child protection clearly a price to be paid for ignoring odd inconsistencies, feelings of discomfort or vague impressions. What involvement with the legal system has done is to push these unfocused bits of evidence out of the files into the memories of the various professionals and so reduced the chances of other people involved with the family being made aware of their existence.

These are major concerns. A patient's right of access to medical records or a defendant's right to defend himself against allegations of child abuse are important principles, but it has to be recognised that at times they may not only conflict directly with therapeutic objectives, but that they inhibit free communication among people involved in protecting children and promoting their welfare. The absence of full records also creates major problems of continuity. Many child psychiatrists, child psychotherapists and child psychologists, even at a senior level, take on 'training' or locum posts of short duration. If information is never recorded in any permanent form it is lost when they move on. Similarly, the illness, death or retirement of a professional involved with the family may leave an enormous gap in knowledge about a child and its family, unless full records have been maintained.

Assessment of parenting capacity

Frequently, judges and magistrates are faced with a very difficult decision involving a 'tug-of-love' between two parents, or parents and foster parents or resulting from repeated incidents of parental neglect or failure to control. At the core of these cases is often the reluctance of the court to take children away from natural parents who have cared for them and with whom they have developed strong bonds.

Faced with such difficult decisions, some courts seek a way out of the dilemma by calling upon a clinic to *assess parenting capacity*. Unfortunately, there appears to be a belief among some lawyers and judges that for a skilled child psychiatrist this is a simple task – a sort of psychological litmus test. You just look the parents over, ask them a few searching questions and out comes the answer: 'yes', they do have parental capacity; 'no' they don't. A lawyer in one case, whose client (the father of the children) had just been released from prison and had not been available for interview at the Clinic went as far as asking a psychiatrist who was about to give expert evidence to carry out an 'on-the-spot' assessment of parental ability outside the courtroom!

Other factors which have increased the courts' need for expert assessments are cultural pluralism and the diversity of family structures. Forty or fifty years ago it may well have been possible to identify criteria which were generally accepted as indicative of good or bad parenting. Children were seen, for example, as needing two heterosexual parents living together in harmony and providing a structured, disciplined but loving environment for the child. Mothers were the primary care-takers, while fathers provided role models for male children and for female children the capacity to develop long-lasting relationships with the opposite sex. Physical punishment was permissible and indeed seen as beneficial to the child, provided that it was not excessive.

Today, in modern post-industrial societies, children live in a wide variety of family structures from extended families to single-parent households with no contact with any other member of the biological family. Many children experience one or more change of family structure during their childhood. The norms of discipline and control and of acceptable behaviour for both parents and children are incredibly diverse. They are determined by cultural factors such as religion, ethnicity and nationality and by socio-economic and geographical considerations. In these circumstances, it is hardly surprising that the judiciary should turn to child psychiatry to provide some clear guidelines based on medico-scientific criteria as to what is and what is not good parenting.

This belief among many lawyers and members of the judiciary that there are indeed medico-scientific answers to questions about parenting capacity is based upon a simplistic view of child welfare, on occasions encouraged by some psychiatrists. It often leads to failures of understanding and disenchantment between court and clinic. Apart from cases involving obvious physical or sexual abuse, assessing parenting ability is fraught with problems. Even when children are inadequately fed and clothed and fail to attend school, this is not necessarily clear evidence of *incapacity* in the parent(s). Conversely, a child may be physically healthy and going to school regularly, but may at the same time have serious behavioural or learning problems, largely caused by harmful parental attitudes.

Children suffer enormously where parents are so self-absorbed and preoccupied that they have no emotional space left for their children. They also suffer when parents treat them as extensions of the self, being unable to allow their children any separate emotional existence. Cases of parents who dress and treat their sons as girls and their daughters as boys in order to fulfil their own emotional needs are notorious. But even here there may well be a *capacity* of the parent(s), with the help of counselling and threat of legal action, to recognise the harm they are causing and to change their treatment of the child. Paradoxically, it is often those cases where the symptoms of parental incapacity are far less dramatic which cause the greatest evaluation problems. For example, it is difficult to convey the harm caused by the subtle and insidious attacks on or the gradual undermining of, a personality.

A fundamental concern for clinic workers in court referrals for assessment relates to the different ways that problems of parenting are presented in court and the significance attached to them by the legal process. To begin with, staff at clinics see from day to day a wide range of family situations where children are suffering from the deficiencies and eccentricities of their parents, but which elude the official attention of social services departments and the courts. It can be disconcerting, therefore, for them to find themselves having to carry out an evaluation of a parent–child relationship where the problems seem relatively minor, simply because the parents are embroiled in some court action.

Generally, when a clinic carries out an assessment, whether or not referred by the court, the overriding question it asks is, 'What does the particular child need to fulfil its potential intellectually, emotionally, psychologically?' Clearly, in order to develop into well-balanced adults with high self-esteem, children need affection and approval, age-appropriate stimulation, adequate physical care, age-appropriate discipline and gradual and appropriate encouragement to separate and acquire autonomy. They also need security and reliable, consistent care-takers in order to develop trust. Assessing these factors takes time and requires considerable skill, despite their apparent simplicity. Given the breadth and complexity of all possible factors, assessments of a particular child's needs and relating these needs to what the parent or parents can offer may seem an impossible task. Moreover, it would appear that any evaluation of this sort would be so interpretive and tenuous as to be subject to all sorts of legal objections of the absence of conclusive proof and lack of objectivity.

Yet, a multi-disciplinary team, such as exists in clinics, is capable of undertaking assessments of children and families using a wide range of skills, psychiatric, psychological, educational, and psycho-therapeutic, including the social context in which the child and family operates and the influences of race, culture, gender and class. When the results of such a multi-faceted diagnostic assessment are combined with a range of theoretical conceptual frameworks using attachment theory, learning theory, systems theory and psychoanalytic theory, the final evaluation has a broad range and depth of understanding. In support of this is a steadily expanding store of research information on child development, resilience factors, predictive factors for long-term mental health and the use of past history in assessing future performance. If all this skill, theory and knowledge can be brought together, then the clinic's child and family mental health team may be able to claim some legitimacy for its views on the child's needs and how best they may be met. However, conveying these views in a straightforward, clear, concise form that makes sense in court may pose considerable problems, as the following specific problems illustrate.

The neglecting parent

One of the major problems in any assessment of parenting capacity is how to untangle the parent from the environment. Where there is a depressed, overwhelmed mother with housing and financial difficulties, for example, how do you establish whether the neglect of the child arises from some deep-rooted psychological problem, which makes it unlikely that the parent will ever be able adequately to care for her child, or whether all would be well if some of the stresses on the mother were reduced or if she could be taught how better to handle them? Often, of course, the parent's behaviour is the result of a complex interaction between psychological and environmental factors. In such cases only monitoring the parent's behaviour over several months or years to see whether or not he or she is able to make constructive use of parental skills training or services designed to relieve some of the strain of parenting is likely to reveal to what extent that parent is *capable*. Yet time is at a premium when the court is demanding an immediate opinion on whether a child should remain in care or return home.

Time is also at a premium in cases involving young children. A child of two and a half, for example, must not be left in a state of limbo, not knowing any consistent parent figures or being separated from a person to whom he or she has become attached. However, providing certainty and security for children is not inconsistent with undertaking a thorough exploration of all possible solutions to the unsatisfactory circumstances in which the children find themselves. All too often a court judgment, based on snap-shots of a particular moment in the child's life and on the superficial gloss of courtroom presentations, seems like a substitute for a proper investigation leading to careful, considered decision-making. Frequently, this is an issue of resource distribution. There seems to be no problem in obtaining funding to pay lawyers to argue the case in court, but in England and Wales Court Welfare Officer Services lack the staff and back-up to carry out the necessary investigative work.

Yet there are occasions when the court–clinic combination appears to work well. These usually concern neglect of an obvious, intentional kind where it has to be brought home to parents that their behaviour is damaging the child. The use of the court's authority backed up with the ultimate threat of removal may well be sufficient in such cases to persuade the parents to change their behaviour.

One such case concerned an eight-year-old girl of a mother but not of her cohabitee. The child was very thin, scantily clad in winter and was made to do the chores in the home and eat in the kitchen while the rest of the family ate in the dining room. This 'Cinderella child' received almost no affection, approval or physical protection. It was an example of painfully obvious neglect to the extent that neighbours and the school both voiced their concern.

The court was presented with a case that was almost self-evident, with the mother and step-father confirming in court their neglect and rejection of the child. The debate consisted of whether there should be total removal or whether the judge could risk leaving the child in the family with some kind of treatment. On the Clinic's recommendation, the court ordered a boarding school placement with the child returning home in the holidays. It also ordered therapeutic work with the family. Over a period of three years the situation improved and the child was able to return to live at home. The total rejection of the child by the mother and step-father had lessened as they became able to 'see' the child as she was rather than regarding her as the unwelcome offspring of her father. The child's social skills and self-esteem had increased so that she also became more responsive to them and rewarding for them.

By contrast, a case where the clinic–court intervention did not work well involved a child who had been severely bruised and was now in the care of social services after an interim care order. The mother, an articulate, intelligent, single parent, worked as a computer programmer. She was very well able to understand the legal issues and fight for her right to keep the child. She asked the court not to confirm the order, but to return the child to her. The history of the mother–child relationship did not, however, inspire confidence. The child had repeatedly been left for long periods each weekday at a day nursery and at weekends with friends, who had become reluctant childminders, while the mother went out. All in all the mother spent little time with her child. Adequate food and clothing for the child were lacking and the child, when assessed by the Clinic, demonstrated patchy development, poor coordination and little in the way of attachments, but an ability to play alone. According to the mother, all the problems were caused by boyfriends who hurt the child, but whenever things went too far she would put the child into care and get rid of the boyfriend.

The Clinic's recommendation, based on past history and a series of interviews and assessment sessions held over several weeks, was for long-term fostering with access and continuing work on the mother–child relationship to see if rehabilitation could be achieved instead of a repeating yo-yo existence for the child. In court the mother presented herself as an extremely competent woman, who had been the innocent victim of her male partners, now fighting for the return of the child whom she loved and cared for. The repeated neglect of the child, the failure of the mother over the years to meet most of her child's needs, was lost from sight in the mother's assurance that she had now got rid of the man who was harming her child. Now, according to her, all would be well. In order to help the child in the future, she was, she assured the judge, prepared to attend the Clinic with her for work on the parent–child relationship.

The court accepted the mother's version of events and allowed the child to return home. The day after the child was returned from care the mother stopped attending the Clinic. Seven months later the child was back in short-term foster care. The Clinic's original assessment of the mother's parenting capacity and motivation to improve her care of her child might just as well not have taken place. The judge, obliged to balance what he saw as the mother's parental rights against possible risks to the child, was so convinced by the mother's articulate courtroom performance on the day that he chose to ignore all the misgivings expressed by Clinic staff in the report to the court.

Low intellectual capacity
Referrals to assess parenting ability often raise serious doubts about the parent's intellectual capacity. This is not in any way to suggest that people with IQs well below average should be prevented from having children or should have their children automatically removed. The problem is rather that in cases where there is severe negligence over a long period, often involving several children, serious concerns may arise as to whether the parent is indeed intellectually capable of learning the skills and sensitivities necessary for adequate parenting. In such cases the court will want to know whether there is any real possibility that the parent will ever be able to care for his or her children, even if he or she is offered help and support.

One example concerned a mother who was known to have had severe learning difficulties at school. She had four children. The two older ones had already been removed from her because of her inability to cope. Now the younger ones, two bright, alert little girls, were in a short-term fostering placement after the nursery had expressed enormous concern about hygiene, feeding, clothing and safety.

The girls were quick and responsive but when they were with the mother they made no demands on her. They kept an eye on her, but turned to each other for support. Mother was slow, depressed and despairing. She used the interviews to talk at length about her own problems. She did not show any concern about the two girls other than to demand their return. She seemed unable to consider how they felt, what they might need from her if they were to return and what might happen in the future – starting school, puberty and adolescence.

It was not easy to untangle how much the mother's poor functioning was due to depression and how much to low intellectual functioning. But her lack of insight into the difficulties, and the impossibility of finding any aspect of her parenting on which she was willing to work or where she acknowledged that she needed help, left very real concerns about the children. The prospects for any change in the child-rearing practices seemed very dim. Given more time and more resources to work with the mother, it might have been possible to hold the family together, but, given her history and her preoccupation with her own problems, there seemed no alternative but to recommend substitute care. Sadly, after the children were received into care, the mother lost all contact with them. They had been fostered at some distance from her home, which made visiting difficult, but the real reason was her resignation to the 'loss' of her daughters. As far as she was concerned, there was no hope of them ever being returned to her. Later the children were freed for adoption.

The court–clinic combination had succeeded in so far as the court was able to act on a full assessment of the mother and the chances of adequate parenting in the future. However, the intervention by social services had ultimately caused the children to lose contact with their only parent because of the lack of substitute care resources within a reasonable distance of the mother's home. This undermined all the good intentions of court, social workers and clinic to provide substitute parenting for the children while maintaining contact with the natural mother.

Parents suffering from mental illness
Parents with mental illness raise even more difficult questions for clinics and the courts. If the mental illness is severe, with the parent exhibiting bizarre behaviour or being dominated by hallucinations or delusions then, even if it does not place children at risk, the situation can create a very strange environment for them to grow up in.

One particularly sad case concerned a mother with a schizo-affective disorder who believed that the milk in her baby's bottle was full of pins and needles and so refused to feed the baby. Each new bottle was supposedly contaminated and the child was losing weight and dehydrating. Medication was unable to reduce the mother's symptoms and so the court had no hesitation in ordering the baby's removal and subsequently freeing for adoption, when the mother's mental condition showed no signs of improving in relation to the baby.

This case, and others like it, appears to be relatively straight-forward, until one examines the complex history of events that led up to the present psychotic episode. Here, the mother already had two children, then aged ten and eight, whom she had brought up quite satisfactorily. She was known to react to stress by psychotic breakdowns, but in between these breakdowns functioned adequately despite the recurrent nature of the illness. Just before this last psychotic breakdown she had been abandoned by the baby's father which had probably triggered the psychotic episode. The two elder children had both gone into foster care after the breakdown, yet it was expected that they would return to the mother once she had recovered.

This kind of case illustrates the difficulties that the courts experience in having to deal with parental mental illness of an unpredictable nature. Sometimes the decisions seem too precipitous and result in the break-up of families. However, at other times the opposite occurs. Here the legal decision-makers may override clinical advice about the likely prognosis for a psychotically ill parent and leave a child in a situation of uncertainty and insecurity. This occurs particularly in cases where a mother, who has been caring single-handedly for her child, has a history of manic-depressive or schizophrenic illness. The courts have tended to regard the mother's illness as a terrible misfortune and may be very reluctant to add further to the mother's misery by permanently depriving her of her child. Clearly, in some cases, long remissions in the psychosis do occur, as in the last case we described where the mother acted normally for long periods. But often it is difficult to predict the length of the remissions or the severity of the relapses. These cases present difficult problems for clinics as well as for courts of deciding what is best for the child. Sympathy for the parent, the desire to treat people fairly, sometimes makes judges and magistrates reluctant to take any decisive action, even where the nature of the mental illness makes rehabilitation impossible for the foreseeable future. The result is often the 'yo-yo child syndrome' where the child is shunted back and forth between parent and substitute carer, until someone, perhaps several years on, says 'enough is enough'.

One example of this yo-yo syndrome concerned a six-year-old boy whose mother was suffering from a manic-depression. The mother had frequent periods in a mental hospital when in a psychotically depressed state. On each occasion the mother agreed to place the child voluntarily in care. This happened thirteen times. The matter went to court twice with the local authority asking for a care order, but the court was unwilling to do more than make a supervision order. On the third occasion, however, the magistrates agreed to the request for a care order and the child was placed in long-term fostering care.

Another case involved a thirteen-year-old boy. Here the mother had been diagnosed as paranoid schizophrenic. She believed that her home was bugged and that she received secret messages via the television. When the child was younger he had experienced several episodes in care, while his mother received in-patient psychiatric treatment. Once again, the history of the legal intervention revealed a marked reluctance by the courts to take any firm steps to provide the boy with stability and security. Although the mother was now able to function out of hospital and the child was adequately clothed and fed, it was the child who was responsible for doing all the shopping. He even collected his mother's child benefit payments. It was only after his persistent failure to attend school and the mother's obvious inability to control his school attendance that the court finally decided to make a care order and the child was placed with foster parents. By then he had effectively missed about two years of school.

We are not suggesting that children should be removed at the slightest indication of mental illness. Our complaint is rather that in this difficult area lawyers and the judiciary tend to apply simple models of mental illness which lead either to their minimising the effects on children, because there is no evidence of physical harm or neglect, or to their exaggerating the immediate danger to the child. One such example of the tendency to exaggerate the danger involved a girl of two and a half who was in short-term care under a provisional order. The parents were separated and the father, with the help of his own mother, had looked after the child since the separation. However, he was admitted to mental hospital suffering from depression. Previously, the only serious episode of depression he had experienced had occurred some eight years ago before his marriage and the birth of the child. He now wanted his daughter to be returned to him as soon as he had recovered from his illness.

The mother, on the other hand, wanted to make a fresh start in life without having the child to care for. The magistrates hearing the case in the lower court decided that the girl was better off with foster parents than with her paternal grandparents. They were clearly concerned for her future with a father who had a history of mental illness. As a result a care order was made in respect of the child.

Subsequently, the father applied to have the care order revoked and for himself, with the help of his parents, again to take on the care of his daughter, but he could not convince the court that he was capable of looking after her. The girl is now with long-term carers with little chance of ever returning to her family. The Clinic's view was that, although this father had indeed been psychiatrically depressed, it was by no means clear that this should have precluded him from permanently looking after his child with the support of his family. This family support, in the experience of clinic workers, is often the decisive factor determining whether it is safe to return a child to a parent with a history of mental illness. It was very unfortunate in this case that the magistrates failed to give sufficient weight to the care available to the child from the extended family. Even if there had been a relapse in the father's illness, there was every reason for believing that the family would have cared for the child.

Snap judgments and the parents' dilemma

Faced with the family situations described in this chapter, the ideal way from a clinical perspective of dealing with the parent–child problems would be far removed from the type of hurried assessments that the court seems to demand of mental health clinics. Typically, it would involve the parent with the children attending a day assessment centre over a considerable period of time in order to assess how the parent and children respond to different situations and to a range of interventions. Only then is it really possible to determine what change might be possible through therapy and support. Clinics are in the business of considering all those small, individual differences that account for human diversity. When they become involved in assessing a family, it looks for all the strengths and weaknesses that can be built upon or compensated for.

The court, however, in its need for immediate answers to yes/no questions – 'Can this mother cope adequately today?' 'Will these children be at risk if they are returned immediately to the home?' – tends, through pressure of time or the distorting effects of cross-examination, to slip into broad generalisations. Parents are often then categorised and evaluated according to simple stereotypes. The complexities, the subtle individual and family differences, tend to be flattened in the legal process.

Moreover, while the answers to these pressing questions may resolve the immediate legal problem and allow the case to be closed, they do not tackle the issue of the long-term welfare of children which lies concealed behind the facade of the legal rhetoric. Would placing them in a new family really be better for them, given all the uncertainty surrounding fostering placements? Would it not be better to defer judgment to see if the parent could be helped sufficiently to allow rehabilitation of the children to take place? Lawyers, judges and magistrates may convince themselves that they have done everything possible by calling for expert opinions on what is best for the child. Yet what in fact they are doing is obliging the so-called experts to carry out an assessment in highly artificial surroundings, to make snap judgments and to defend their provisional and tenuous conclusions in court as if they were definitive statements for furthering the child's best interests.

The combination of the court's decision-making power and the clinics' supposed expertise may create an impossible dilemma for parents who are aware of the problems they are experiencing in providing adequate care for the children. If they admit these problems in court, they risk losing the children in the adversarial contest. The pressure from the legal situation combined with the advice from their own lawyer is, therefore, likely to cause them to deny or minimise these difficulties. Yet by doing so they risk falling into the clinical trap of being branded as parents who refuse to admit the existence of problems and who, therefore, are closed to any possibility of help through therapy or training.

A high proportion of parents referred to a clinic by the court will take a defensive stance when interviewed, denying that there is anything seriously wrong with the children or blaming circumstances or others for any abuse that has taken place. In most of these referrals the constraints imposed by the courts do not allow sufficient time to go beyond this defensive position. The case goes back to court without any of the underlying problems being exposed and the parents continue their public denial of these problems in the hope that there will be insufficient countervailing evidence and that the court will accept their version of events.

Occasionally, however, for one reason or another the assessment will go on for some time and the parents will attend a clinic on several occasions or the parents' lawyer may advise against an adversarial stance. In such cases the parents may let the mask fall and allow the clinical assessors to see their feelings of despair and inadequacy and to share their fears for their children's safety and security. The problem then often becomes one of trying to convince a court that it should allow time for work to be undertaken with the parents and to convince the social services to provide resources for help and support. Where this has been allowed to happen the results have often proved positive for parents and children, but often the change of heart comes too late. By this time the children are already in substitute care and it is virtually impossible for everyone to change and move in the opposite direction.

Summing up

1. We have given an account of some of the general problems that occur when clinics become involved in court cases. Despite their shared interest in promoting the welfare of the child, there exists a wide gulf between the methodological approach of courts and lawyers and that of the clinical workers towards determining children's needs and the best way of responding to them.

2. We have seen how the issue of confidentiality may interfere with the therapeutic work of clinics by undermining trust between the patient and a therapist who can give no reliable assurance that what passes between them will be private. We have also seen how therapists may be obliged to reveal their clinical notes to the court, so damaging often beyond repair the possibility of any further therapy with the patient, and we have examined the unintended consequences of court subpoenas demanding production of clinical records – the notes which say very little and which are of minimal use to those who treat the patient at a later date.

3. We have gone on to remark how it seems unavoidable for the legal process to reduce complex issues to simple choices to be made on the basis of 'the facts' presented on a particular day or particular days – the 'snap-shot' approach, as we have called it. Clinics, by contrast, attempt over what may be a lengthy period to unravel a mass of complex information obtained from various external sources and from tests and interviews that their staff conduct. They try to identify the children's needs and assess the capabilities of the family to meet those needs. They consider how strengths might be built upon and weaknesses contained. As far as it is possible, they try to predict how the child will fare in the future in different situations.

4. This is not to suggest that clinics are always 'right' and the court, where it disagrees with the clinic's view, always 'wrong'. Clinical assessments are far from infallible. Parents may change their behaviour contrary to all past-indicators. Sometimes, to coin a phrase, the most carefully laid clinical plans come to nought, or are frustrated by unforeseen events. Sometimes things go so badly

wrong that in retrospect the clinical intervention served no useful purpose. There are bound to be failures whatever system of assessment is undertaken, such is the contingent nature of human existence. What we have attempted to explain in this chapter is the way that the failures of law are of a different kind from the failures of clinics. The failures of law tend to arise from pressured decision-making, the shorthand classification of people and their problems into simple stereotypes, the seduction of the well-argued case or the convincing performance of a witness. In court there is a proneness for judges and magistrates to be swayed by immediate impressions and to discount or underplay the importance of lengthy written reports.

5. The nature of legal training and practice makes it difficult for courts to rid themselves of the need to attribute blame and to promote fairness and justice for the innocent. This on occasions leads to decisions being founded on sympathy for a helpless victim and the avoidance of the 'injustice' of removing children from a blameless parent. There is no doubt that laws which allow for the sudden 'disqualification' of parents through the removal of all rights, including keeping in contact with their children, and policies which provide a system of substitute care which systematically excludes parents, encourage the type of courtroom battle which is all too familiar to English and American lawyers where the issue is (or is perceived to be) that of winning or losing a child.

6. We have also described how these different approaches of court and clinic may place parents in an impossible situation. The court often appears to require parents to deny that they have any problems and to present the public image of people who are quite capable of meeting their children's needs. Clinics, on the other hand, often interpret denial and unrealistic claims of parents as a failure to recognise problems as they really are and as symptoms of an inability to accept help and of an unwillingness to change. In the next two chapters we take the different approaches of court and clinic into two specific areas, that of matrimonial disputes and child sexual abuse.

Further reading

Official inquiry reports into incidents of child abuse

A Child in Trust: the Report of the Panel of Inquiry into the Circumstances Surrounding the Death of Jasmine Beckford (the London Borough of Brent, 1985).

Report of the Committee of Inquiry into the Care and Supervision Provided in Relation to Maria Colwell (HMSO, 1974).

Report of the Inquiry into Child Abuse in Cleveland 1987 (HMSO, 1988).

Mentally ill parents

'Children of Mentally Ill Parents' by Elizabeth Rice in *Problems in Child Care* edited by E. Rice, M. Ekdahl and L. Miller (Behavioural Publications, 1971).

'Psychosis in Parents: Mental Illness as a Problem for the Family' by Elizabeth Irvine, *British Journal of Psychiatric Social Work* (1991) 6, pp. 21–6.

Assessment and working with parents

Good Enough Parenting – A Framework for Assessment by Margaret Alcock and Richard White (British Association of Adoption and Fostering, 1985).

Marital Violence by N. Johnson (Routledge, 1985).

The Needs of Parents. Practice and Policy in Parent Education by G. Pugh and E. De'Ath (Macmillan, 1984).

Parenting Breakdown: The Making and Breaking of Intergenerational Links by D. Quinton and M. Rutter (Avebury, 1989).

Working with Parents. Framework for Collaboration by Cliff Cunningham and Hilton Davis (Open University Press, 1985).

4

The Court as Marital Battleground

It is relatively rare, at least in the United Kingdom, for marital conflicts to lead to courtroom battles over children. It is even more rare for mental health clinics to be involved. Certainly, the psychiatrists at the Tavistock Clinic receive a steady trickle of requests from divorced or divorcing parents (or their lawyers) to assess their parenting capacity and the relationship with their children with a view to supporting their case for custody; but, as a matter of policy, these are usually refused on the basis that the clinical workers will not take sides, but will only become involved if requested to do so by the court.

Judges or the Official Solicitor, who acts for children in the High Court, call upon clinical services only when the situation is so complex or so fraught that the Court Welfare Officer Service cannot cope. The cases that we recount in this chapter, therefore, are in no way typical of divorce cases in general. Yet the one factor that is common to all of them – the extreme suffering of the children – is, we suspect, not confined to the few cases that are referred to mental health clinics. Only when that suffering is linked to allegations by one former partner against the other and these allegations are refuted and met with counter-allegations is the issue likely to result in a fierce legal contest which raises matters of clinical judgement.

Since the ability to fight a legal case in the High Court requires either private means or a level of articulateness high enough to convince both one's lawyer and the legal aid authority that one has a case worth fighting, it is perhaps not too surprising that the families involved are usually middle class and well educated. Another reason may be that fathers from this social milieu are much more likely than their working-class counterparts to demand to play an important part in their children's lives after the marital breakdown. Whatever the reason, the client population from matrimonial cases contrasts sharply with that of child abuse and neglect cases referred to the Clinic by social services departments.

Few people are able to behave totally rationally and unselfishly at times of crisis, uncertainty and great unhappiness in their life. Yet, with the help of conciliation services, counselling and sensitive assistance from specialist matrimonial lawyers, an increasing number of separating and divorcing parents have been able to travel a considerable way along the road to the ideals of continuing parental responsibility and the least possible disruption to the lives of their children. In these 'sensible' divorces the law's role is limited. It may do little more than encourage parents to work out together their own arrangements for the continuation of their parenting roles and set out in very general terms what kind of arrangements are likely to meet the court's approval.

These 'sensible' divorces rarely cause serious problems for either court or clinic. Neither do those cases where one parent (usually the father) disappears entirely from the scene. Parental absence, particularly where preceded by bitter conflict, may have adverse medium- and long-term effects on the children who may well be referred to a clinic at some later stage in their development. In the short-term, however, the family tends to stabilise around the remaining parent and, in some cases, his or her new partner. The only immediate problem for the court is how to get the disappearing father to pay for his children's upkeep.

Excluding the 'mad' or 'wicked' parent

The situations which raise all sorts of difficulties for both court and clinic are those where one parent (usually but not always the mother) makes allegations of cruelty, insanity and/or child sexual abuse against the other in an attempt to vilify and exclude the former partner from any future contact with the children. Where court and clinic are able to act together, each using the other's skills, some cases which appear stuck and impossible can move.

In a middle-class family, a mother who left her husband, taking her daughter, was insistent that he was domineering and controlling her and the child and that she could never return. The father questioned the mother's sanity and the school raised concerns over the over-close relationship between father and daughter. The parents were shocked to learn from the Clinic's assessment of their daughter's distress and longing for *both* her parents. When the case returned to court the parents accepted joint custody and frequent access to father. They also accepted counselling sessions as a parental couple. None of this would have been possible without the authority of the law, and the court for its part was able to use the Clinic's assessment to promote the child's well-being. The barrister and solicitor for each parent played an important role in shifting the adults from warring marital partners to parents of their child, so reinforcing the Clinic's work.

A far worse situation arises in those cases where the children themselves become caught up in a shared world of perceiving the absent parent as an evil or dangerous person to be excluded at all costs. This occurred in a case which was originally referred to the Clinic by a divorce court welfare officer. The welfare officer asked for an assessment of the children, aged eight and twelve, who were living with their mother. How troubled were they by the fighting between their parents? What arrangements for custody and access would be best for them?

The mother did not want to have anything to do with the Clinic and so appointments were frequently missed. This failure to keep appointments inevitably aroused some antagonism at the Clinic as missed appointments are particularly frustrating for already over-loaded staff. It was only after her solicitor advised her that it was in her interests to cooperate that she started attending appointments on time – by this time it was quite hard for the Clinic staff to hold on to their objectivity in their assessment.

Mother and children were seen together and there was general agreement among them that the only problem was the husband and his persistent demands to see his children. He was described by mother as mad, sick and in need of treatment. He was also perceived by them as evil in that he was able to convince people (the judge and probably now the psychiatrist carrying out the assessment) that he was a caring, concerned parent. This, according to the mother and children, was a total deception. The husband/father merely wanted to 'exert power', 'to control', he was 'unable to let go' because of his fear of losing face. When interviewed on her own the mother expressed her concern that she should not lose the independence that she had fought so hard to win for herself. Often, in the past, her autonomy had been undermined by her husband until in the end she felt obliged to leave. Now she was determined to remove 'that man' from her world. There was no reason as far as she could see for him to have access to the children. She claimed that, as a father, he had been very peripheral to their lives, rarely taking any interest or showing any concern. For him the children were just possessions which now he could not bear to lose.

The father was seen on his own. He appeared articulate, distressed and concerned for the children and their future develop-ment if they were to remain physically with their mother and emotionally wrapped up with her. Father appeared reasonable and careful not to criticise or run down his former wife too much. But he repeated endlessly his wish to be part of his children's lives.

The children, when interviewed individually, pleaded with the psychiatrist never to see their father again. They wanted to be left alone. If their father really loved them as he was pretending to do, then he would know that the best thing he could do would be to go away, vanish, die. Although this was repeated in a cold, hard manner, the children appeared vulnerable and troubled. One of the girls was particularly hard and ruthless. She declared herself to be indifferent, untouched and getting on with her life, but reports from her school showed that her performance had deteriorated. The other child was tearful and sad. She had become very clinging and sucked her thumb.

Attempts at an access appointment as part of the assessment resulted in very distressing scenes with the children being contemptuous and vicious to their father. The father attempted to remind the children of the good times – outings, fun, activities they had enjoyed together – by producing photos of them all together and letters from close friends or relatives they no longer saw. The children dismissed these with cruel disdain. As the session progressed, the father found it increasingly difficult to retain his air of reasonableness and attacked his ex-wife for brain-washing the children, controlling their thoughts and feelings.

After the interviews the battle raged on between the parents, supported by their solicitors right up to the court hearing. The outcome of the hearing was an order for some access in favour of the father to take place in the presence of a third party, with social services to try to provide a neutral venue and an escort to assist the children. These visits never took place. The mother, who had care and control, managed to have them all cancelled by claiming that the children were ill or had gone away to stay with friends. On other occasions the children simply did not turn up.

In cases of this kind what happens in the future often depends upon the father's persistence. One such case came back to court every year for review with no progress having been made. The children would not see their father and refused to accept his letters, postcards or pocket money. Six years later, his ex-wife wanted help in looking after the children, now in adolescence, and the father is now seeing them. This was a mother who previously had threatened to have her former husband murdered if he ever contacted the children.

Another father, whose former wife had refused him access to his daughter, waited two and a half years before bringing the matter back to court for review. Supervised access was ordered. The father sent letters and cards, but still no access took place, as the child leapt out of a moving car to avoid seeing her father. He has now remarried and has had a baby. He refuses to pay any maintenance, but lets his first wife and daughter know where he can be contacted, leaving it to them to take the initiative.

It would be wrong to give the impression that it is only mothers who are unable to restrain their anger and resentment over the past relationship and its breakdown and allow these feelings to dominate their view of the parenting capacities of the other. The reason that in most of the cases referred to the Clinic it is mothers who are causing the difficulties is simply that mothers are much more likely to have care and control and therefore be in a position to manipulate the children and control access. Fathers, however, do frequently represent their former partner as 'evil' or 'insane' and attempt to persuade the court and Clinic staff of her corrupting influence on the children.

In one case a father referred his two children, aged nine and seven, to the Clinic for help. He was concerned about the distress which he claimed his wife was causing them. He had lived with his wife in the ground floor flat of a large house belonging to his mother. All had gone well at first, but as the children were born relationships started to become difficult. There were disagreements between his wife and mother over child-rearing. He tended to side with his mother, which left his wife feeling increasingly undermined and vulnerable. When her own mother died she became depressed and lacking in confidence. Her doctor prescribed antidepressants, but they were of little help. The father's mother took over more and more of the child care. Finally, the children's mother confronted him with the stark choice – either he found different accommodation for the family or she would leave him. In fact, she did leave and the referral to the Clinic came at the point when her solicitor was writing requesting access pending an application for custody of the children.

The father and children were insistent that the mother was mentally ill. They were concerned that she should have treatment. The father could see no reason for leaving his present home where the arrangements were 'excellent' and the children were 'settled'. The children were upset about their mother's 'breakdown' and were reluctant to see her because she would talk about them coming to live with her.

The meetings arranged between husband and wife proved to be painful. He suggested that she should have treatment and, when 'well' could return to the household. She was insistent that she wanted a family independent of his mother. Over time their positions became entrenched. After a meeting at which the hopelessness of the situation became apparent, she tried to commit suicide. This confirmed for the husband that continued contact with her would be damaging for the children. When the case came to court the wife was awarded supervised access.

The children were extremely worried about their mother, but had been persuaded by their father into seeing her as 'a very sick woman'. When interviewed, the elder child, a girl, launched into an attack on psychiatrists who could not make her mother better 'so that we could all live together'. All would be well if her mother was 'better', that is, restored to what she was like before.

At family meetings arranged at the Clinic the grandmother was a powerful presence. She knew how families should function and how children should be brought up. The husband was quite unable to challenge her. The clear message was pity and compassion for 'poor, sick mother' just as long as she remained away. The children seemed subdued, flat and lifeless. They were having nightmares. It was suggested that the children have sessions at the Clinic to help them think about their relationships with their parents. The father would not go along with the suggestion.

The court order for supervised access remained in force but the children always had 'very good reasons' for finding each proposed visit 'inconvenient'. Subsequently the mother took the case back to court because she had been denied access. The court decided that the children could not be forced to see their mother against their will.

In the face of extreme parental intransigence the courts are quite powerless to promote the children's well-being. Any attempt to enforce access orders by imprisoning the mother for contempt or handing over the children to the father is likely to increase the children's problems rather than relieve them. In practical terms the most effective measure the courts can order is for access to be supervised. What then happens is that the social services or a voluntary agency supervises parental visits. But even this will not work where the parent who has care and control is determined that no access will take place and has succeeded in turning the children against the other parent.

This is not to suggest that the Clinic is any more successful. The most that clinics can do in such cases is to counsel the parents about the effects of their actions and offer sessions for the children, where they would be able to explore their own feelings, and to distinguish them from those of their parents. Whether this is likely to help depends very much on the willingness of both parents to cooperate – often no more than a pious hope. At least, however, it does not bring even greater distress to the children.

The father as sexual abuser

A mother decided that the children's access visits to her former husband should end. She had become convinced that her children, aged five and eight, had been sexually abused. The father contested in court the refusal to allow access and the issue was referred to the Clinic by a High Court judge.

When interviewed, the mother was volatile and violently hostile to her former husband. She said that she would rather die than let her children visit him. Father appeared articulate, thoughtful and surprisingly uncritical of his ex-wife. He saw her as a reasonable mother, but a difficult wife. He wanted to resume contact with his children. The two children seemed very troubled. They appeared unable to give a coherent account of their lives. Neither of them was prepared to talk about any sexual abuse by their father. Both had enormous learning difficulties and behavioural problems. They were described in the Clinic's report to the court as out of control, a danger to themselves and to others.

Following the Clinic's recommendation, the court ordered temporary, separate foster home placements for the children for the purposes of a full assessment. At the foster homes they became even more disturbed and bizarre in their behaviour. They were quite unable to function at school. After a short period, they began to speak about the sexual abuse, both anal and oral, that their father had inflicted on them. So the mother's allegations had been correct and the Clinic's scepticism of the mother's allegations had been proved to be unfounded.

The court excluded the father entirely from the children's lives. This, however, did not prevent him applying for access, which he still does at regular intervals, but without success. He writes letters and sends presents to the children through the social services department.

Such allegations of sexual abuse during the course of divorce proceedings have increased substantially in recent years. Perhaps this is only to be expected given the amount of media coverage of child sexual abuse. Added to this is the fact that the courts are more and more reluctant to exclude a parent from his or her child except where continued contact is likely to put the child at risk of harm. This means that branding a parent as a sex abuser (in the case of fathers) or someone who associates with a sex abuser (in the case of mothers) may be the only sure way of using the law's authority to keep that parent out of the child's life.

These accusations in the middle of divorce proceedings present even greater difficulties for court and clinic than allegations of parental madness or wickedness. As in child care and protection cases, whenever sexual abuse is mentioned, the ringing of the alarm bells drowns almost everything else concerning the children's welfare. For the 'accused' parent, the court hearing offers an opportunity both to clear his name and to revenge himself against the accusations of his former partner. This opportunity is often seized with alacrity by that parent and his lawyers. Concern for the child is then swamped by the courtroom battle.

In another custody and access dispute the Clinic workers were again sceptical. A six-year-old girl told her mother that her father had sexually abused her during her access visits. She described how he had 'fondled her private parts'. Mother, who was very keen to exclude father from her daughter's life, immediately terminated access. Father then made the child a ward of court.

When interviewed at the Clinic the child was clear in repeating very closely the allegations of abuse as described by mother (to social services and police) but there was a robotic quality to her descriptions. She was adamant that she did not want to see her father ever again. She was very controlling and expected her wishes and her orders to be complied with; she was unable to play spontaneously and freely. Everything was done with meticulous care – a drawing showed a mummy rabbit and girl babies; 'boys are no good', she said, 'Don't need daddies'.

The mother was totally bound up with her daughter and frantic to keep father out. The intensity of the feelings was overwhelming. When they were interviewed together, every question to the child was answered by mother, who spoke all the time of 'we' and 'us'. The child had no thoughts, feelings, ideas, responses of her own. Mother came from a very sad and deprived background. Father was a more articulate and cooperative person, expressing concern for the mental health of his child. He wanted her removed from the mother and totally denied any sexual contact between him and his daughter.

From the start the court hearing focused on whether the abuse had occurred or not – everything seemed to concentrate upon the guilt or innocence of the father. The child and her needs seemed to become entirely lost from sight. The lack of conclusive proof of sexual abuse by the father had the effect of discounting any possibility of any abuse having occurred. The energy of the court was absorbed and dissipated by the issue of the father's guilt or innocence. No one seemed interested in the child and what had happened to her, and what sort of life she would lead. It was as if nobody in court could remember that they were there because of concerns over the child's welfare. In the event she remained with mother, who was awarded care and control. Access to the father continued. The Clinic's suggestions of further work with the parents to help them understand their child's needs and with the child to clarify her own thoughts and feelings were not taken up.

By contrast, in some other cases, where no sexual abuse has occurred, the mere glimpse of behaviour which could be interpreted as sexual or sexualising may be sufficient to ring the alarm bells and result in the court zealously ordering protective measures for the child. In one case a child aged ten, of recently divorced parents, seemed to be tired and unhappy and was struggling at school. She mentioned to her mother something about 'sleeping with' her father, during staying access visits. The mother immediately terminated all access. The father then decided to fight this in the court.

The Clinic was asked to assess the children and parents. Mother and her new partner were seen. They appeared capable and competent, articulate and very hostile to father. When the girl was interviewed, she explained that she had lain in father's bed watching television until she fell asleep. Father seemed immature, naive and volatile. He failed to see why he should keep his daughter out of his bed or move the television out of his bedroom.

The child was sad and unhappy, she felt excluded by her mother and the mother's new partner and she was worried about and felt responsible for her father. However, she said that she did not want to sleep in her father's bed on access visits. 'It's not right.' Yet there was no evidence of inappropriate physical contact between father and child.

The father was so determined to defy his ex-wife and maintain his existing close relationship with his daughter that he failed entirely to grasp that the child needed to be treated as a person in her own right. She was growing up and was moving towards puberty. She revealed during her interview that the very close relationship with her father made her feel stifled and uncomfortable, but said that she did not want to tell him about her feelings as this would hurt him. When the father was interviewed at the Clinic, it was explained to him how his daughter felt. His reaction was one of disbelief. If she really felt that way, she would tell him herself.

It was a sad and frustrating case from everyone's perspective. If the child had been referred to the Clinic by the parents or school for reasons other than sexual abuse within the context of a matrimonial dispute, there might well have been the possibility of focusing on the child's needs. At the centre of the problem was a troubled child, a mother preoccupied by her relationship with her new partner and her wish to establish a new life, obliterating her past unhappy marriage and a father clinging on to his daughter partly to protect her from the disruption caused by the marital breakdown, but also as a consequence of his unresolved feelings for his former wife. Work with the family to enable the daughter to express her feelings and with the parents to respect her autonomy and to separate their feelings for her from the resentment and hostility they felt towards each other might have produced positive results. As it was, none of this was possible.

The legal framework determined the issues on which the Clinic was forced to concentrate. Any possibility of work with the family was thwarted by the fact that an allegation of sexual abuse had been made and had to be defended to the hilt. The Clinic's report for the court spelt out clearly the child's dilemma and explained that what was required was work with the adults. The hearing, however, centred around the sexual abuse allegation. The judge saw that there was a risk of sexual abuse, failing to recognise that the real problem lay elsewhere. He ordered that staying access should end, as the Clinic had recommended. Contrary to the Clinic's advice, however, he insisted that all future access to the child should be supervised by a close relative. Mother felt she had lost the case because her former husband would continue seeing the child. Father felt that he had lost because access visits were to be restricted and supervised. The real loser, however, was the child. Subsequently, the Clinic attempted to follow up the decision by writing to both parents offering them the possibility of sessions to discuss their relationship with their daughter. Neither of them responded. In this case the combination of court and clinic had failed to persuade the parents to put the child's interests before their own.

Problems of the law's response

By setting itself up as an arbiter of 'objective truth' in matrimonial disputes, the law presents itself to warring parents as having the power to do justice between them by, among other things, discovering the 'truth' about allegations made by one party against the other. The fact that 'objective truth' may be very difficult to prove, particularly in sexual abuse cases involving young children, is a major obstacle to the law achieving its objectives.

Another problem is that the justice that the law offers is often no more than a *paper justice*. Victories tend to be empty and meaningless in so far as they relate to future parent–child relationships. A father and his lawyers may congratulate themselves outside the courtroom at having resisted his wife's allegations of sexual abuse and so 'put the record straight'. Yet, even if the court has awarded him access, the chances of his now being able to enjoy a close relationship with his children will, if anything, have been diminished by the court proceedings and his determination to clear his name. Moreover, the relentless struggle to establish 'the truth' in the courtroom is likely to have exacerbated the antagonism between the parents and reduced considerably the chances of cooperation in the future.

Where the allegations fail, there is a strong tendency by child care agencies and the courts to treat the absence of conclusive proof as a rejection of the allegation and therefore as an indication that no remedial action is necessary. Where some evidence exists of 'inappropriate parental behaviour', as in the last case we described, the court may well want to protect the child, but finds that all it can do is to deploy clumsy and heavy-handed remedies, such as banning a parent from seeing his children or demanding severe restrictions on access. Even if the court orders are obeyed, such remedies, rather than encouraging parents to cooperate or to seek help, are more likely to have the effect of driving the parents into even more entrenched positions.

There is a feeling among some lawyers and judges that the most effective way of dealing with warring parents is to subject them to the authority of the judge, whose findings of fact will be respected and whose orders will be obeyed. This may work with 'reasonable' parents, but the kind of intransigent parents who are determined to fight tooth and nail to protect their children from what they see as their 'mad', or 'evil' or 'sick' former partner are unlikely to be pulled into line by figures in authority. The same applies to those parents who are set on clearing their name by proving to the world that they are not guilty of their spouse's accusations. Threats of imprisonment for contempt for removing the children are likely to produce either more intransigence or a forced compliance which generates more resentment and hostility.

In these extreme, but by no means rare, cases any benefit for the child of seeing the non-custodial parent is likely to be offset by one or both parents attempting to sabotage or undermine the relationship of the child with the other parent. In the few cases where intransigent parents eventually come round to adopting a more reasonable attitude, it is usually time and not the court or the legal process that can claim the credit. Yet, despite these obvious limitations on its effectiveness and its often negative impact on the relationships between parent and child and between the parents, the legal system seems unable to escape from its obligation to take on the responsibility of handling matrimonial disputes over children and of making Solomon-like judgments about which parent or which combination of parents is best suited to provide for the child's future welfare.

The legislators for England and Wales have made a brave

attempt to avoid the systematic use of the courts to regulate the relationship between parents and children whenever marriages break down. In the Children Act 1989 there is an assumption that, despite the failure of the marriage, parental responsibilities will continue to operate. Instead of fighting over formal custody and access (which no longer exist as legal concepts in English law), parents will, it is hoped, make arrangements between themselves and resolve any conflict over where the child should live and over the nature and frequency of visits without having to drag the issue before the courts.

This may well avoid some of those contested cases which have more to do with one parent seeking to obtain recognition of their credentials as a child-carer than the promotion of children's interests. However, it is unlikely on its own to make any difference to those cases where the irrationality, hostility and selfishness of one or both parents rules out any compromise and forces the issue before the courts. Short of denying to parents the right to litigate, it is difficult to see how, within the context of the existing system, such contested hearings and the harm they cause to children could be avoided. One fundamental improvement would be for judges and magistrates hearing such cases to concentrate attention firmly on the issue of the children, and rule as inadmissible any allegations made with the sole intention of undermining the parenting capacity of the other party. The court's role would be to promote arrangements for the child's future welfare and not to determine on the accuracy of each parent's allegations against the other. It would, however, take an experienced, knowledgeable and forceful judge to transform the adversarial nature of such proceedings into an enquiry into what was best for the child.

Well-run conciliation and mediation schemes probably offer a better forum than courts for such exercises in welfare promotion. However, they are even more impotent than courts when faced with intransigent parents, since they do not make authoritative decisions or have the power to enforce those decisions. We shall take up this problem again in the final chapter when we examine possible reforms to the existing decision-making process.

Further reading

Effects of separation and divorce on children's development
Children in the Middle by Ann Mitchell (Tavistock, 1984).
Divorce Matters by J. Bourgoyne, R. Ormrod and M. Richards (Penguin, 1987).
Marriage, Divorce, Remarriage by Andrew Cherlin (Harvard University Press, 1981).

Mate and Stalemate: Working with Marital Problems in a Social Services Department by J. Mattinson and I. Sinclair (Basil Blackwell, 1979).

Second Chances by J. Wallerstein and J. Blakeslee (Banton Press, 1989).

Separation, Divorce and the Development of Children by M. Richards and S. Dyson (Child Care and Development Group, Cambridge, 1982).

Separation, Divorce and Development of Children: A Review, Report for the Department of Health and Social Security (HMSO, 1982).

Surviving the Break-up by J. Wallerstein and J. Kelly, (Grant McIntyre, 1981).

Divorce and the courts

In the Child's Best Interests: Divorce Welfare Officers and Court, Search for a Settlement by Christopher Clulow and Christopher Vincent (Tavistock Publications, 1987).

5

Court and Clinic: Different Perceptions of Child Sexual Abuse

Nothing has brought about more fundamental and far-reaching changes affecting both the work of the mental health clinic with children and families and its relations with the court than the 'discovery' in the 1980s of child sexual abuse. Before this, the court–clinic relationship was reasonably clear. Children who were failing to thrive or who exhibited abnormal or excessively withdrawn behaviour would be referred to the clinic by schools, social services and, occasionally, courts for assessments or therapy. The assessments, as we have described in Chapter 3, would attempt to identify the children's emotional needs, evaluate the ability of different potential care-takers to meet those needs and help to plan for the children's future.

As we have shown, this process is by no means free of problems in the court–clinic relationship, but such problems tend to result from the different conceptual and procedural approaches of lawyers and mental health professionals to the issues raised by the case. The boundaries between law and mental health remained relatively well demarcated. While prosecutions, place of safety orders and court hearings would from time to time interrupt therapy programmes, the legal system did not seriously interfere with the Tavistock Clinic's work. There was no attempt by legal professionals to impose their procedures and values on the operation of the Clinic. However, the discovery of child sexual abuse has changed all this.

In part, the changes have resulted from public anxiety over child sexual abuse. More than any other form of abuse it touches the raw nerve of people's sensitivities, which the popular press and broadcasting media have not been slow to exploit. Where it occurs within the home it seems to threaten the very foundations of family life, transgressing the incest taboo and undermining both the notion of childhood innocence and the protective, caring role of parents towards their children. It arouses people's fear, anger, guilt and disgust to a much greater degree than other forms of abuse. For a parent to hit a child is, to many people, understandable, but to use children as objects for adult sexual gratification is seen as so monstrous as to defy all rational understanding. The crude, gut-response of many to child sexual abuse is to demand that the children be removed immediately and the perpetrators be prosecuted with a view to locking them up for a very long time. These attitudes tend to be encouraged by the tabloid press and in the broadcasting media. They inevitably influence what judges and magistrates come to identify as 'public opinion'. However, if the evidence against the parents turns out to be less convincing than it seemed originally, public and media tend to switch allegiances. Now the family must be protected against unwarranted interference by the state and above all by 'busy-body social workers'. Once again, the courts tend to reflect these attitudes.

Yet it is too easy to accept the line of some academic commentators and interpret the strength of public feeling over child sexual abuse merely as a 'moral panic' which should be resisted by sensible legal and mental health professionals. To do so is in part to ignore the very real suffering of children who find themselves caught up in an emotional whirlwind with no prospect of a soft and happy landing. These children do need help, but the overriding problem for professional workers is how to offer that help without causing even more harm to the child. Only too often professional intervention seems to superimpose its own form of abuse over and above that already perpetrated against the child – and all in the name of child protection.

The first obstacle to any offer of help is simply that of identifying the sexually abused child. Despite the claims of some professionals, it is in most cases extremely difficult to obtain unambiguous physical evidence of the sexual abuse of young children. In the majority of cases the identification of sexual abuse therefore has to rely on the interpretation of indirect evidence from the child's behaviour or on verbal disclosure.

In young preschool children indicators of sexual abuse include symptoms such as bed-wetting or soiling, vulval or vaginal soreness in girls, soreness at the base of the penis in boys and soreness of the anus in both sexes. These young children may also complain of 'tummy ache'. As for behavioural symptoms, they may be preoccupied with masturbation or engage in obviously sexualised play. Less obvious behavioural signs of possible sexual abuse, indicating a struggle to make sense of sexual experiences, may include an inability to learn or living in a highly vivid fantasy world which seems to them more real than the actual world.

In primary school children there are no conclusive behavioural symptoms. These children may complain of 'headaches' as well as 'tummy aches'. They may also talk of tiredness and bad dreams. Often these children are first noticed because they are isolated or friendless or because they engage in bullying or inappropriately friendly behaviour, coming very close and seeking too much physical contact so that those around them feel uncomfortable. Some of the children have a problem with undressing for sport activities.

Secondary school children have similar symptoms, but in addition they may start running away from home, absconding from school, attempting suicide, engaging in alcohol or solvent abuse, in promiscuous sexual activities or develop anorexia nervosa. Some may become pregnant as the result of abuse.

Most of these behavioural symptoms, of course, apply to a wide range of disturbances in children. None can be said to be specific only to sexual abuse. In the absence of clear physical symptoms or corroborative evidence, some disclosure by the child is necessary in order to identify the cause of the behavioural problem. This raises considerable problems of detection wherever the sexual abuse occurs within the privacy of the home. So furtive are the sexual acts and so secretive are the participants that even other members of the family living in the same household may not know what is going on. Not only are child sexual abusers able to conceal their acts by a web of secrecy, they are also often themselves a victim of its compulsive and addictive nature. As such child sexual abuse is in many ways much closer to drug and alcohol addiction than to 'normal' physical child abuse and neglect. Moreover, although all types of child abuse involve a victim, in sexual abuse the victim may well have a deep emotional dependency upon the perpetrator which results in a paralysis, an inability to break free from or even to talk about the abuse. In some cases the perpetrator may also threaten the victim with all kinds of terrible consequences, if the abuse is revealed.

For staff at the Clinic these difficulties have serious and far-reaching repercussions for any attempt to provide therapy for children and families which do not exist in cases of 'normal' physical abuse or neglect. Even where the perpetrator has previously admitted the abuse, the secretive, addictive nature of sexual behaviour may place the child in an impossible situation of having to lie to the therapist that no further abuse is taking place because of threats and emotional blackmail from the perpetrator. Quite apart from the problems caused by any legal intervention that may take place, therefore, child sexual abuse presents considerable problems for the Clinic's therapeutic function.

Sexual abuse also presents major difficulties for the legal system, but of a different nature from those it presents to clinics. They arise in the main from the fact that Anglo-American jurisdictions tend to require only a strong suspicion of sexual abuse for initial emergency action to remove the child. Yet, for a successful prosecution or for intervention to supplant long-term parental authority and allow planning for the child's future, there must be very clear evidence of abuse having occurred. The court's criterion for intervention rests on proof of sexual abuse in a form which satisfies the legal rules of evidence and procedure. For the law, sexual abuse constitutes an illegal act which may give rise to a criminal prosecution or to the loss of parental rights. As such the case must be properly proved and the defendant must be given every opportunity to challenge the evidence. For mental health professionals, on the other hand, disturbed or distressed behaviour in a child is a sufficient ground for believing that some intervention may be necessary if only to understand the causes of the child's behaviour and to offer help to the child and family. The ways that these two very different approaches may conflict with one another is the subject of this chapter.

The quest for evidence

After the 'discovery' of child sexual abuse, any clinical interview with children becomes potential evidence for legal action. Because of the ever-present prospect of a police prosecution or child protection proceedings, any hint of sexual abuse means that all normal therapeutic procedures must end. If, for example, a child is likely to begin to 'disclose' during an interview at the Clinic, that interview may well have to be brought to a close in order that the disclosure may be made in front of the video camera. The clinical justification for this procedure is that it will probably be much better for the child to have the disclosure in the form of a video recording to be available for an expert witness called by any party to the case than to subject the child to repeated interviews. Yet closing an interview or changing its style may be extremely disruptive for children. Some children also find the technology of video cameras, microphones and one-way mirrors extremely unsettling. It is all too easy for the interviewer to feel the need to press the child, to play 'hunt the truth' games, searching all the time for more clarification, more details, more confirmation. The point can be reached when the length of the interview and the level of stress are themselves abusive to the child.

If the child has felt able to reveal what has been going on, the whole paraphernalia of the law and the courts has to be faced. Instead of working to help the child overcome the effects of the abuse, the Clinic staff can find themselves involved in preparing the child for court and in discussions about which of them will be called to give evidence. In cases involving more than one child,

such as sex abuse rings, any attempt to undertake joint therapy
sessions will be likely to be thwarted by the police or by the
solicitor advising social services. The need to present a convincing
case in court overrides help for the children. If the children are
known to have communicated with one another before the court
hearing, their credibility as witnesses may well be suspect and the
prosecution may fail as a result.

Embarrassing and humiliating experiences when required to give
expert evidence in court have taught Clinic staff to become very
careful in what they say in interview, once there is a suspicion of
sexual abuse. One careless slip can lead to accusations of asking
'leading questions' and to the child's disclosure being negated as
evidence in court. The freedom to listen to the child, observing
play activity and analysing drawings in a relaxed, spontaneous
manner is lost.

Frequently, sexually abused children are relieved to talk and to
be told that what has been happening is wrong but that it is not
their fault. But this relief may be short-lived when panic takes
over at the prospect of the family being broken up. Will father or
step-father be sent away? Where will mother get money from?
The children beg you to keep quiet. They want the abuse to stop,
but do not want the family destroyed. In part this may be an
overreaction resulting from the effects of the abuse itself – the
'parentification' of the child, who has been forced to take on the
responsibility of a parent. But, given the clumsy way the legal
system operates, there may be a strong element of realism in the
child's fears.

Following disclosure, the inevitable confrontation between police
and social services on the one side and the family on the other
almost invariably leads to hostile and defensive attitudes among
those who have been caring for the child. Families who up to that
point had seemed to cooperate with the Clinic and other helping
agencies withdraw the child from therapy. The demands of the
legal process then take over with the result that so much time and
energy goes into determining whether abuse has occurred or not
that the more thoughtful work with the family, the attempt to
retain their confidence and involvement, falls by the wayside. The
family often feels so threatened that any admission of any kind is
impossible. Everything is denied; all problems are discounted.

If the parents are subsequently vindicated in court of sexually
abusing their child, the chance of further therapeutic work with the
family is virtually non-existent. People accused of such monstrous
behaviour are hardly likely to ask for psychiatric help, for to do
so might be seen as an acknowledgement that they have problems,

as an admission that the allegations against them might have been correct after all.

Faced with the probable consequences of reporting a suspected case of child sexual abuse, clinical workers are often caught in two minds. Should they 'rescue the child' whom they strongly suspect has been sexually abused? Should they on the other hand apply a rule of optimism? The knowledge of the painful and distressing consequences that are likely to flow from any involvement of the legal system may at times lead workers to allow themselves not to recognise possible indicators of sexual abuse.

Given the prospect of immediate interference from police and lawyers in their therapeutic work, of having to defend their clinical role in court against accusations of 'putting words in the child's mouth' and of making false accusations against the parents, it is not surprising that many child and family mental health professionals prefer not to become involved. Some of these simply retreat as far as possible from any work which involves child sexual abuse. Not only does this add to the pressure for those who remain, but it also denies to children and families the services of people with just those skills that are needed for comprehensive, multi-disciplinary assessments which are such an important part of a clinic's work.

Court referrals in sexual abuse cases

When a case comes to court with allegations, but no unambiguous proof, of sexual abuse, some judges will call upon a clinic to carry out a psychiatric assessment of the child. They may even demand from the clinic answers to specific questions, such as 'Has X been the victim of sexual abuse?' 'What has been the nature and frequency of such abuse?' 'Who was the perpetrator of the abuse?' In one case a High Court judge ordered that the Clinic should limit its assessment to one interview with the child and should not see any other member of the family. He asked to know on the basis of that one interview whether or not the child had been sexually abused and the identity of the perpetrator. The Clinic, after much soul-searching, decided that it could not carry out the court's demand.

Such unrealistic and uncomprehending demands by courts create anxiety and some resentment at the Clinic. There is anxiety over the burden of responsibility that is placed on the shoulders of the psychiatrist who is to carry out the assessment and report to the court. There is much resentment among some mental health professionals at the way in which the court is using the clinic for legal purposes with little or no appreciation of its therapeutic function. It is as if the legal system sees clinics as scientific laboratories whose sole purpose is to carry out tests on children to find out whether a crime has been committed and, if so, by whom. Furthermore, there is often little appreciation of the limitations of psychiatric and psychological assessments. In those cases where the child does not disclose abuse during the assessment, but where lingering doubts remain, there is a distinct feeling in the courtroom that somehow the clinic and the psychiatrist have failed to do the job that was required of them.

The reality is that, in the absence of unambiguous physical damage or traces of semen or blood, child sexual abuse against young children is extremely difficult to prove. Contrary to popular belief, most young children presented with anatomically correct dolls do not immediately pick them up and go on to reveal details of the abuse they have suffered. The most frightened and inhibited children may refuse to have anything to do with the dolls. Other children may make very general references to what happens sexually between men, women and children, but decline to mention names or give any details of abusive acts. Those few children who launch fluently into florid descriptions of what happened to them at the hands of the abuser sometimes give the impression of having been carefully rehearsed. Others appear to have repeated their 'story' so many times that they now want to get the business of telling it over as quickly as possible. A fairly common pattern of events in cases which reach the Clinic as the result of court referrals is for a young child to have made some spontaneous comment about sexual abuse to someone they have known for a long time such as a teacher or a relative. Once the initial exposure has taken place and the social work and law machines have launched into action, the child frequently closes up and refuses to talk again about the abuse. S(he) may even go so far as to deny that the abuse ever took place, contradicting the earlier, spontaneous statement. It is at this point that the Clinic may be called upon by the judge, social services department or the lawyer representing the child to carry out an assessment to establish whether or not the abuse actually occurred.

Faced with a frightened and confused child, for the interviewing psychiatrist to coax a disclosure, that will stand up in court, is no easy task. First, the interviewer has to win the child's trust to the point when (s)he will feel secure enough to play, draw and talk spontaneously in the interviewer's presence. This obviously takes time and with the judge and lawyers breathing down one's neck, waiting for the answer to their legal questions, the pressure can be overwhelming. Secondly, even where trust is achieved and the child feels free to express thoughts and feelings, these do not come out in the form of neatly packaged statements. Rather they emerge in coded form through drawings and play activities, which have to be interpreted by the interviewer. These interpretations will often then be subjected to the scrutiny of the lawyers and to cross-examination in court.

Children's drawings

The drawings of children are a form of communication that needs to be taken seriously. Often children use this indirect form of communication to reveal aspects of themselves and their world. The messages that young children convey may often be confused and ambivalent, mixing fantasy with reality. One child, aged eight, for example, drew a heavily pregnant woman with the comment, 'there's a baby in there.' She also drew herself with a swollen abdomen, babies in cots, babies in beds, babies everywhere on the page. Previously the child had told her teacher that her dad had abused her. Her mother worked as a childminder so there were babies going in and out of the home. Was this preoccupation with babies and reproduction an indication of sexual abuse or was it simply a description of her home environment or of her jealousy for the babies who monopolised her mother's attention?

Drawings are never on their own diagnostic, but certain drawings do appear to recur so often among children who have been sexually abused that their appearance alerts Clinic workers to the possibility of such abuse. Only rarely have they been drawn by children who have not been sexually abused. Once a child has presented such a drawing, the therapist will attempt to explore with the child over a number of sessions the areas of conflict and pain in that child's life in order to bring these out into the open.

Children may, for example, draw objects with obvious phallic connotations, such as trees with very stubby crowns or branches (Figure 1) or lighthouses flashing (Figure 2). Once these drawings appear the worker will usually encourage the child to talk about their families, babysitter, neighbours or people at school. Sometimes in that session or later sessions they will go on to discuss physical contact such as touching, tickling and cuddling and details of abuse may emerge.

There has been some indication that where children draw spiders and webs (Figure 3) they tend to go on to talk about being trapped or pinned down. They may reveal that they have been physically restrained in some way by someone stronger than them and, from

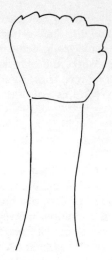

Figure 1

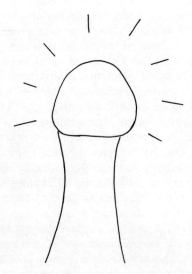

Figure 2

time to time, details of sexual abuse emerge.

Sometimes children will accentuate various parts of an adult's anatomy. It seemed strange for example, for a child to draw her father with enormous sausage-shaped fingers (Figure 4) as this was drawing attention to a bodily feature not usually accentuated by children. In sessions with the child over the following few months

Figure 3

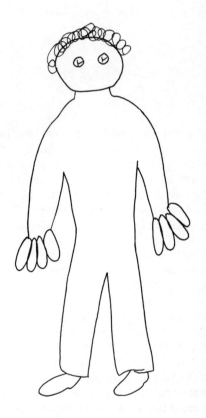

Figure 4

Figure 5

she gradually became able to talk about her father and his holding and touching of her until she was finally able to disclose sexual abuse – digital penetration followed by penile penetration during which she was held down to prevent resistance.

The child who drew the face with the open mouth that filled the house and a small figure beside the house (Figure 5) was at her next visit to the Clinic able to talk about shouting mouths and mouths that had things forced into them. She then went on to reveal oral and anal abuse at the hands of her father.

A simple request to 'Draw your family' may produce very revealing results for a wide variety of mental health problems. The relative size of the figures and their arrangements provides clues as to the child's perspective which may then be explored. The small, distant father, for instance, may suggest that he is a very peripheral figure who is absent a good deal or a divorced and distant father (Figure 6). However, it may also be an indication that the child would like the father to be small and distant. Exploring this with the child can open up the conversation to such areas as anger, crossness, naughtiness of adults or children, touching, smacking etc. It may also enable the child to talk about abuse.

Where the child draws the male adult figure with a prominent fifth member and states this to be a penis or 'willy' (Figure 7), then there are serious grounds for concerns about possible sexual abuse.

Figure 6

Such drawings, however, are relatively uncommon among children. Where the male genitals are displaced, being represented, for example, as a prominent nose or hair bow (Figure 8), this gives rise to similar concerns. Again, it must be emphasised that there is no clear diagnostic evidence that the child has been abused, only an indication that the area of sexual abuse needs exploring. On occasions it has subsequently transpired that the misplaced protrusion was simply a quirk in the child's drawing with no sinister undertones.

A few children find it impossible, despite enormous encouragement to draw the lower half of a person's body (Figure 9). This is always an indication that the relationship with that person is in some way significant. It is important then to try to explore with the child the nature of the relationship with that person and what happens when they are together.

Figure 7

Figure 8

Children's play and behaviour during interview

Children's play may also provide indications of past sexual abuse.
Toy animals, both wild and domestic, or pipe-cleaner dolls may be
given to children who will be asked to play out scenes with them.
The children may use them to depict violence or obviously

Figure 9

rhythmic sexual activity. This is not on its own evidence of sexual abuse, for the children may have witnessed sex videos or seen their parents making love. One child made a toy bull repeatedly mount other animals and dolls. She then declared how her bottom used to get sore and how it hurt. However, sexual abuse in her case was never proved to the satisfaction of the court.

Some children are very explicit in their play. They may, for instance, make themselves a house or a bed by moving around the furniture. They then proceed to re-enact their sexual experiences. Other children go through the motions of re-enacting their sexual experiences. Some tend to do this in a self-absorbed way, while others try to involve the interviewer by climbing onto laps and trying to touch breasts or undo trouser zips. If allowed to remain on the interviewer's lap, they may try to masturbate themselves astride the interviewer's legs. If they are put down, they may masturbate against furniture. All this can be very distressing and difficult to handle. It is also difficult to untangle how much of this behaviour reflects what they have discovered through exploring their own bodies, how much through mutual exploration with friends or siblings, how much through watching videos and how much through actual physical contact at the hands of an adult. For the interviewer, the unravelling of behaviour from experience without making the interview itself abusive to the child is a major problem.

Life would be much easier if there were some clear relationship between the nature of the children's play and the likelihood of abuse having occurred. Unfortunately, it is not possible to assume such a relationship. Some children engage in highly explicit sexual behaviour, but have not been sexually abused. Others are much less explicit in their play. All they do is play monsters, ghosts, snakes and crocodiles explaining how these creatures come out at night to attack, biting and hurting. Yet, as happened in one case, where a little girl talked about crocodiles coming out of the lavatory bowl to bite her bottom, this play was a clue to the fact that abuse had indeed taken place.

Tying the appropriate legal label to the child

Once sexual abuse has been alleged, there is a tendency for all subsequent legal action concerning the child and family to depend, not upon the child's needs, but upon the strength of the evidence of the abuse. Children are classified and dealt with, therefore, according to legal criteria, which may be very different from the Clinic's criteria for intervention and the nature of the treatment necessary to help the child.

A girl, aged four, was referred to the Clinic by a judge for assessment. During the course of four assessment sessions the child produced violent outbursts which the interviewers found strange and very worrying. She also disclosed that she had experienced oral, anal and vaginal sexual abuse. The culprit seemed to have been the father, but he was adamant that he had not touched her. For the interviewers, the sexual abuse seemed to be the least of the little girl's problems. She was extremely troubled and disturbed, seeing and hearing things that did not exist. She was controlling and domineering to such an extent that she was difficult to be with. She was convinced that she could do whatever she chose including being able to fly. Just keeping her safe was a problem. Also her anger presented a risk to those around her. She said repeatedly that she missed her father who did the bulk of the child care. She wet and soiled herself because of her terror of 'the monsters in the toilet who will bite her'. This child was in desperate need of help regardless of actual occurrence of abuse.

Her mother came from a very deprived and distressing background, being brought up by substitute carers from the age of eight and leaving for London when she was sixteen. She had married the father, who was a good deal older than her, because she thought that he would provide security and stability. She appeared distraught and at the same time furious with the child, with nothing good to say about her. She wanted to care for her daughter, but could not bear having the child near her and could not stand any physical contact. The marriage had broken down some months earlier, but the father had maintained regular contact with the child.

This was a child who was crying out for help. It was clear that her problems arose from her very disturbed state and were impossible to manage in the present home situation. Those who assessed her at the Clinic were unanimous in their recommendation that she needed a period of substitute care together with intensive therapy. However, the court hearing in the High Court focused on the abuse and the circumstances in which the father had left the home. The court seemed preoccupied almost entirely with the issue of whether sexual abuse had in fact occurred. This father contested the case and it was unresolved despite many hours of evidence and argument. Consequently the child's level of disturbance and hence her needs were entirely lost from view. The mother became very defensive and resistant to any offers of therapy for the child, which she regarded as a veiled attack on her parenting capacity. Lawyers for both the mother and social services together succeeded in creating a feeling in court that all would be fine provided that the mother and her child received some social work support. The court would not accept that the child had enormous emotional difficulties that needed specialist help.

The issue became simply one of 'was this child competent to give evidence so that the father could be prosecuted'. This was the only aspect of the girl's serious psychological problems which seemed to interest the court. With the father strenuously denying the abuse, the absence of sufficient evidence to prosecute meant, it appeared, that there were no grounds for the court to remove the child from the home or to order treatment. In fact, the court ordered that the girl should remain with her mother who was left to handle her own feelings and those of the child and to care for her other children.

Within six months the girl's school was raising the alarm. The child was climbing onto the roof and threatening to jump, smearing faeces on the walls and attacking other children. The mother lurched from one crisis to another. Fortunately, because this child had been made a ward of court the case could be returned immediately to the High Court for a review hearing. This would not have happened if the proceedings had taken place in the lower court, where there was no automatic review process and the only way for the case to have returned to court would have been on a fresh application on the part of social services.

When the matter came back to the High Court both social services and the judge at last took notice of the Clinic's reports and accepted the recommendations for therapeutic residential boarding school, for family work and intensive treatment. The child was put into the care of the local authority who placed her in a residential therapeutic community. Two years later she is less disturbed, but is still very fragile.

Long-standing problems with little change

In some cases, there may have been concerns for some time about the family and its functioning but nothing sufficiently concrete has emerged to warrant legal intervention. Frequently, such a family is very reluctant to accept help or to turn to anyone for advice. In one such case an eight-year-old girl, after a health education lesson in school on the danger of talking to strangers, told her teacher straight out, 'My Daddy has sexually abused me.' Social services were contacted, visited the school and, with the mother's consent, placed the child in a foster home. The father was confronted with the allegation and denied any contact with his daughter. Nevertheless, he offered to leave the home so that the daughter could return.

This is what happened, but the mother then accused her daughter of lying. She wanted her husband, the sole bread-winner, back. All members of the family now agreed that the daughter was just 'attention seeking'. According to the family, she was upset because her mother was at the hospital visiting the grandmother, and father was frequently out. There were no physical signs and nothing could be discovered by interviewing the girl or anyone else in the family. During sessions at the Clinic with the girl and with her brother, the difficulties in the parents' marriage (father had another woman) and the learning problems both children had in school became apparent.

The court hearing was brief. There was no evidence and therefore no case. The long-term concerns and more general mental health problems were not given any airing. The professionals 'lost' and the family, as winners, made very clear that they did not need any help, since 'there were no problems'. Subsequent telephone calls from the school expressing anxiety and concern to social services and the Clinic produced considerable frustration on all sides as there was little that could be done. The parents saw no reason to cooperate and no need for help.

A similar case of 'inadequate evidence' concerned a six-year-old girl who was reported by her school as displaying a range of disturbing behaviours, including excessive masturbation using objects, obsessive spinning in the playground, touching boy's genitals and a total lack of concentration. The child's father, who lived apart from her mother, admitted playing with his daughter's nipples, but denied any sexual abuse. The parents agreed to a doll interview, which ended inconclusively, although the professionals present had a strong feeling that the child had been sexually abused. The mother not only denied the abuse, but refused to accept that her daughter had any problems. Then the child's younger sister complained to a teacher that her father had touched her in the vaginal area. This provoked a dramatic reaction from social services who took both children into care on an emergency order. Once again, however, there was no conclusive evidence of abuse.

The case alleging the abuse of both children was due to go before the lower court mainly on the strength of the video evidence of a doll interview. However, the reaction of the four lawyers involved in a pre-hearing showing of the video was so hostile – they claimed that the interview was abusive to the child – that social services stopped the case and made the children wards of court. With the case pending in the High Court, the father went abroad and the behaviour of the elder child improved. However, when he returned to the country, her over-sexualised, excited behaviour returned. Mother nevertheless continued to discount all these indications that the father had been abusing his daughters. She continued to want him to return to her. Eventually, there was an irreversible separation between the mother and the father. The mother began living with another man and some time later the younger child revealed to him that it had been her uncle, the mother's brother, who had been abusing her. And so it goes on, with no way of knowing whether there is any truth in the allegations.

We would not go so far as to suggest that without firm evidence of sexual abuse no legal action can ever be taken to improve the situation of a child whose mental health is being harmed. What we are saying rather is that when any allegations of sexual abuse are made they become the focus of attention and the legal case rests or falls on the strength of the evidence supporting the allegations. If there is insufficient evidence to warrant a finding of sexual abuse having been committed, reports by mental health professionals of the child's mental distress and confusion as evidenced by abnormal behaviour tend to be ignored. In some cases, however, the family circumstances may be so unsatisfactory that the court will intervene despite the absence of clear evidence of sexual abuse.

In one such case social services were extremely concerned about neglect, failure to thrive and delayed development in a family of three children. Numerous agencies had been involved, trying to support the parents and get them to change their style of parenting, but to no avail. The family had huge rent arrears, as a result of which they were evicted and put into bed and breakfast accommodation. When the little girl, aged three, was taken to the doctor for ear-ache, she was found to have a sore, red vulva. Social services then called a case conference to consider whether the father had sexually abused her. This prompted a referral to the Clinic, which revealed that all three children were below the third centile in weight and height and growth had ceased for one girl. On the strength of this evidence social services applied to the magistrates' court and all three were taken into care on interim care orders.

At the hearing of the care proceedings no firm evidence of actual sexual abuse was produced, although it was revealed that the home conditions were such that it was never very clear who slept where and who touched whom. Certainly, the children had probably witnessed sexual intercourse and had watched sex videos. There had been a chaotic boundary-less relationship with babysitters, family friends and extended family. The children masturbated themselves and each other.

The outcome was that the three children remained in short-term foster care for fourteen months. Attempts at rehabilitation with the parents failed, as the parents were unable to sustain regular contact and to provide meals and adequate sleeping arrangements. The children were moved to long-term foster parents after an application for reversion of the care order. At the hearing the parents fought very hard to keep the children, but when they 'lost', contact between them and their children lasted only a further six months.

The effects of legal intervention

Sexual abuse within families, because of its secretive and compulsive nature, is different from other forms of child abuse. These differences call for close control of the relationship between the abused child and the abuser or alleged abuser. There is no argument between court and clinic about the need for such control. It is the way in which this need is identified at present by the legal system and, where identified, the way in which control is achieved that create frustration and despair among mental health professionals. So often clinics are left watching as helpless bystanders while the situation unfolds. Any indication of sexual abuse from young children themselves or from doctors examining them – and the children risk being removed from their families on emergency orders. The belief seems to prevail among hard-pressed social workers who apply for emergency orders and the judges and magistrates granting them that to leave the children a day longer and expose them to the risk of further abuse may cause such additional harm that something has to be done immediately. In most instances, however, the abuse will have been going on for some time and the child will have already suffered such psychological damage that a reasonable delay to allow for careful planning, and perhaps attempts to find ways of protecting the child with the cooperation of the parents, would be unlikely to lead to further harm.

The sudden removal of the children at once creates a situation of confrontation between the professionals and the parents. Unless a clinic's mental health team is very careful, it may be drawn into the battle on the side of the professionals. They become 'the enemy' in the eyes of the family. Any chance for the psychiatrists or therapists at the clinic to attempt a more subtle approach of discussion and persuasion is sabotaged by fear and anxiety to protect the children. These children can be suddenly pitch-forked into new homes and new schools, often taking with them few of their clothes and favourite toys. Where the child was undergoing therapy, that therapy can be suddenly terminated.

The sad irony from the clinical perspective is that in a high proportion of these 'commando raids' to save children from sexual abusers the children are returned home some weeks later either because of insufficient evidence or because the perpetrator has (supposedly) left home. Now the clinic finds itself on the other side of the fence having serious reservations about the arrangements for the children's protection. The sudden removal from the family, apart from causing a terrible shock to the children, in many cases serves to unite unstable parents in the fight against the professionals for the return of their children. These parents and stepparents will often go to considerable lengths to present themselves in court as a cohesive, functioning family. The professionals who know the family well are only too aware that, despite the attractive image of cohesion offered by the family's lawyer, this united front is very likely to disintegrate as soon as the courtroom battle is over. Yet there is no way of proving this in court. Workers at the clinic have to sit back and wait patiently, knowing that the children are back in a situation where they are suffering and aware that the legal action has ruled out any possibility of therapeutic work with the child and family.

On some occasions all these misgivings prove to be wrong and somehow the family manages to sort out its problems in ways which protect the child. This happened, for example, in the case of a mother who, some time after the court hearing, changed her mind about her husband, having denied in court any possibility that he could have abused the children. She excluded her husband from the home and allowed the Clinic to undertake work with the children. In other families the mother succeeds in protecting the child without excluding the perpetrator from the home. In many of the cases, however, the children's problems continue unabated with the legal proceedings having made matters worse for the children than they were before. Only when some further crisis occurs is there a chance that the children's suffering can again become the focus of attention for the legal process.

Discussion

In this chapter we have described what we believe to be serious problems in using the courts to promote the welfare of sexually abused children. For reasons which have more to do with the nature of the legal system than with individual judges or lawyers, the courts tend to become preoccupied with establishing 'the facts', whether the abuse occurred, who was the perpetrator, than with finding constructive solutions to the child's emotional problems as perceived by clinical workers. Where young children are involved, 'the facts' are all too often not available in a form that satisfies legal requirements. All one has is indirect disclosures which point to something deeply disturbing and distressing having happened to that child. To make any kind of therapeutic intervention dependent upon proving in court specific acts of sexual abuse is to ignore the needs of the child.

This does not mean that we advocate the arbitrary removal of children or the suspension or transfer of parental rights without due process of law. Nor are we denying that the courts can in some instances play an important role in the protection of children. What we are demanding rather is that the focus of attention should be the child and not 'the facts'. Unfortunately, allegations of sexual abuse cause the stakes to become so high and emotions so highly charged that, whenever there is ambiguity or uncertainty in the evidence, it is almost impossible for court hearings to avoid the adversarial mode with the parents vehemently denying the abuse and social workers insisting it did indeed occur. It is significant that the most successful cases of clinic–court cooperation take place only when the child's predicament forces the matter back into court. By this time the initial battle over 'the facts', which predominates at the first hearing, has ceased to be an issue and the court can at last concentrate its attentions on the child.

The legal solutions to this problem which concentrate upon

making court procedures less formal and adversarial, improving judges', magistrates' and lawyers' understanding of child welfare issues and importing into the court expert knowledge in the form of psychiatrists and guardians *ad litem* are unlikely to overcome the almost irresistible orientation of court hearings towards determining questions of right and wrong, truth and falsehood. Despite the worthy efforts of legislators and reformers, something more is needed if the child's future welfare is not to be sacrificed on the altar of the legal rights of adult litigants. What this something should be will be discussed in Chapters 7 and 8.

The other disturbing issue associated with the legal system's handling of child sexual abuse cases is that of secondary harm caused to the child victim through the operation of the legal process itself. There has been much discussion about the obvious trauma for children of giving evidence. However, the outcome of the case is probably more important in its effects on the long-term mental health of the child. Some commentators have argued that the trial and condemnation of a sex abuser could well be therapeutic for the child in that his or her version of events has been accepted and a public statement has been made to the effect that it is the adult and not the child who was to blame for what happened. This may be so, but the opposite is also true. When the evidence is insufficient for a conviction or a civil order to protect the child, whatever the niceties of the strict legal position, the message to the child-victim is likely to be that his or her story has been rejected and the adult vindicated. The child is the one who has caused so much trouble for the family.

It could be argued that there is some justification for placing a child in this situation, where it is a matter of prosecuting for serious sex offences. The condemnation of such crimes and the labelling of the offender may be necessary for the public interest. The same, however, could hardly be said to be true of civil proceedings which develop into a contest where the prize can be an official version of the truth vindicating or condemning one or other of the parties. The result of such contests amounts only too often to what Tilman Furniss, one of the leading European specialists on child sexual abuse and a former psychiatrist at the Tavistock Clinic, has described as 'abuse-promoting child protection'.

Further reading

The Abusing Family by Blair Justice and Rita Justice, rev. edn (Useful Books, 1990).
Child Sexual Abuse by Jean La Fontaine (ESRC, 1988).

Child Sexual Abuse within the Family, Assessment and Treatment by Arnon
   Bentovim, Anne Elton, Judy Hildebrand, Marianne Tranter and Eileen Vizard
   (Wright, 1988).
The Common Secret: Sexual Abuse of Children and Adolescents by Ruth Kempe
   and Henry Kempe (Freeman, 1984).
*Hilary's Trial: The Elizabeth Morgan Case – a Child's Ordeal in the American
   Legal System* by Jonathan Groner (Simon and Schuster, 1991).
Intervening in Child Sexual Abuse edited by K. Murray and D. Gough (Scottish
   Academic Press, 1991).
*The Multi-professional Handbook of Child Sexual Abuse: Integrated Management,
   Therapy and Legal Intervention* by Tilman Furniss (Routledge, 1991).

6

Experts, Lawyers and the Court Experience

Going to court

I remember in particular one Juvenile Court which I attended on behalf of a mother who was likely to lose the two children remaining in her care. The older two children had already been removed and placed in care with a view to adoption. It was a long drive across London; when I eventually found the court there was no parking. There was no coffee for sale, the toilet for all the women lawyers, witnesses and professionals was a separate outhouse, smelly, with the rain coming in, and no paper or soap. The court waiting area was a room with four wooden benches. We all crammed in there; anyone wanting to talk in private went outside and stood in the rain. The child care hearings were in parallel with the criminal hearings so there were bleary-eyed people smelling of drink, a violent young man with his police escorts, and the child care cases. The atmosphere was tense and the room smelt. (A child psychiatrist from the Clinic)

Few courts are quite as bad as this, although in England and Wales lack of investment in the legal system has meant that there are no buildings reserved exclusively for family cases. In the lower courts, hearings of child protection cases often take place in the same buildings as criminal trials. In some courthouses, facilities are so scarce that the same courtroom may be used in the morning for criminal sentencing and in the afternoon for deciding the arrangements for a father to see his children.

The atmosphere in court and the way in which the case is conducted will be determined in part by the physical environment of the courtroom. Imagine, for example, rows of high-backed benches with the lawyers sitting in the first two rows and the parents, social workers, expert witnesses in small groups behind their advocate. From a side door at the front of the courtroom the judge emerges. Everyone shuffles to their feet and the lawyers bow their heads in reverence. As a concession to the fact that this is a 'domestic' case and not a criminal trial, the judge and barristers do not wear wigs, but the formality of the setting, the way that people are grouped into separate factions and the extreme reverence with which the lawyers treat the judge and each other are enough to convince outsiders that they are entering the special world of lawyers where normal, everyday relations are suspended and natural behaviour gives way to performance of the roles allocated by the legal system.

For expert witnesses from the Clinic, the performance starts when they are called to take their place in the witness box. For those new to legal work this is 'the moment of truth'. One child psychiatrist from the Clinic described his first appearance in court as 'terrifying'. Another told how, even after giving expert evidence several times, she still experiences an 'overwhelming sense of guilt' as soon as she steps into the witness box. For her this guilt does not arise from the belief that she has done wrong. It comes rather from an awareness that she is being forced into a position of having to make a definitive statement about what is right for the child at that particular time:

> I feel very anxious, particularly about the fact that most of our evidence, in my view, is not hard evidence, it's soft evidence, it's a matter of opinion and however hard I try to be as certain as I can as a human being that what I'm saying is in the best interest of the children and the families concerned, I find the whole idea of having to make definitive statements of this kind particularly difficult.

Another psychiatrist from the Clinic reported that time and time again he found himself saying to lawyers who were cross-examining him, 'But it's not like that; it's more subtle. There can be arguments on both sides. Things aren't black and white; certainly not in this field.'

Other expert witnesses, by contrast, appear to take the whole thing in their stride. One child psychiatrist from the Clinic told, for example, of how the respect that he as a doctor received in court made him feel 'both excited and powerful'. This, he admitted, may not necessarily have been a good thing but, nevertheless, he chastised those of his colleagues who balked at going to court and submitting their views to public scrutiny:

> I think that's part of our role, we are public figures, we're better paid and as such we have to translate this mysterious task into a language which judges, and journalists and lawyers can understand and I think that's part of what we're paid for actually.

Yet, as we have seen in earlier chapters, it is not simply a matter of 'translating' but rather of fitting the complexities of interpersonal relationships and the diversity of influences on people's behaviour into the conceptual framework which the law imposes. It also involves learning to play 'the courtroom game'. This comes with experience. According to one psychiatrist from the Clinic:

> when I started I felt I was only allowed to answer the questions with a 'yes/no' answer. I now feel a bit freer to say, 'yes, but . . . ' and put an argument . . . At the beginning I was a bit worried that things weren't getting across and that I couldn't find a way of making a point, unless I was asked it. Probably from watching too much Perry Mason!

Some expert witnesses learn to play the courtroom game very effectively. They become socialised into the role of giving their opinion with confidence and conviction and defending it against the fiercest cross-examination.

The danger of this socialisation process is often recognised by expert witnesses in children's cases but, if they want to secure what they believe to be the best outcome for the child, there is little they can do to avoid it. They are obliged to 'play the legal game' and employ courtroom techniques in order to achieve their objectives. The problem is that, unless they are very careful to distance themselves from their courtroom performance, they run the risk of substituting legal definitions of issues and legal values for their clinical judgement.

One child psychiatrist gave as an example a case where a mother with a history of incompetence and neglect was applying for custody of her child. While the psychiatrist was in favour of continuing contact between child and mother, she was anxious that the child should not be returned to the mother's care. This psychiatrist said that she found herself 'driven into the position of saying she's an absolutely appalling mother' and of 'totally annihilating her' by undertaking a 'character assassination' in order to prevent any possibility of the child going home to a mother who was unable to cope with him. In adopting such an extreme stance in her expert evidence the psychiatrist realised that she ran the risk of the court cutting off access entirely – an outcome which she considered to be detrimental to the child's interests. The situation, she explained, required her to act strategically in court because she feared that anything said in the mother's favour would be seized upon by the mother's barrister and used as an argument for the child returning home.

It is a short step from here to psychological experts accepting as correct and normal the use of tactical ploys to obtain from the court what they think is right for a child. What may have begun as a scientific exercise in the use of specialist skills, knowledge and experience to make an assessment from the available information becomes a courtroom contest to be played according to the legal rules.

Making the expert accountable

The ideal of putting experts in the witness box to make them accountable for their methods and their decisions is rarely achieved in practice. In English courts psychiatrists are more likely to be treated with reverence than have their expert opinions scrutinised.

Where challenges to an expert's evidence do occur, it is the witness's ability to stand up to cross-examination that tends to be tested rather than the validity of his or her assessment procedures or the validity of his or her recommendations for the child's future well-being.

A common tactic among lawyers is to ask the psychiatric expert witness if s(he) is familiar with a particular research study or a book or article written by any well-known professor of paediatrics or child psychiatry. If the witness admits to being ignorant of the study or its results, s(he) immediately loses credibility. The lawyer then goes on to summarise the study's conclusions or reads a passage from the learned professor's writings, in order to show that these conflict with the witness's recommendations in the present case. Let us say, for example, that the research purports to show that children who are separated from their mother at a certain age are more likely to suffer mental disorders in adulthood than children from intact families. This would be used by the lawyer as evidence that it would be wrong to separate the particular child in this case from its mother.

The expert witness is then left with the difficult task of explaining why s(he) does not feel bound by the findings of the research study or the views of the eminent professor. The study may have been methodologically unsound; the professor's views may be controversial. It may not be valid to apply previous research findings or general pronouncements on what is right or wrong for children to the present case. There may be special factors in this case which distinguish it from those studied in the research or the learned professor's views may have limited relevance to the present situation.

Another tactical ploy is to play one psychiatrist off against another. In one case involving a psychiatrist from the Clinic, the lawyer for prospective adoptive parents was very insistent that an eminent psychiatrist, Dr X, had recommended that it was in the interests of children who were about to be adopted that visits from the natural parents should end and that there was no reason why this general principle should not be followed in this case. Here a nine-year-old boy was in his third foster placement. The previous placement, also for prospective adoption, had broken down. Now the biological mother had taken the opportunity of the court hearing to ask for her access visits, terminated some four years earlier, to be reinstated. The child was eager to be adopted and anxious about the outcome of the court hearing, but nevertheless wanted to see his mother. It took considerable determination and perseverance on the part of the Clinic's psychiatrist to resist the lawyer's arguments, reinforced by the seemingly unassailable authority of Dr X and hold out for some access to the mother, which the psychiatrist felt would be helpful to the child.

Another example indicates how general statements by psychiatric experts may be applied to particular cases as if they constituted something resembling a legal precedent from the House of Lords or Supreme Court. This case concerned an abused child who was so disturbed that the intimacy and close contact of family life seven days a week and twenty-four hours a day would, according to the Clinic's assessment, have been likely to be very stressful for the child. Rather than risk repeated failures in family placements, the Clinic recommended a period of residential treatment. This was strongly contested in court on the basis that a certain Dr Y had expressed his total opposition to an 'institutional placement'. For him only a family could answer a child's needs. The fact that in this case the little girl concerned was extremely disturbed and had suffered previous breakdowns of family placement was not sufficient to change his view. The court accepted Dr Y's authoritative views and the child was placed in a family. Six months and another failed foster family placement later, Dr Y conceded that in this particular case a residential setting was after all the better solution.

It is important to see what is happening here in terms of different disciplines and different procedures for testing the validity of people's opinions. What the psychiatrist is in fact being asked to do is to treat the results of a research study or the pronouncements of an eminent professor in the way that a lawyer would deal with a previous authoritative decision of a higher court which conflicts with the arguments that the lawyer is putting forward.

Those experts who are experienced in the ways of the courtroom are likely to give a much better account of themselves than the first-timers. Some psychiatric experts, for example, become very adept at warding off attacks on their opinions. One psychiatrist at the Clinic told how in one case involving the sadistic sexual abuse of children a barrister asked him in cross-examination whether he was familiar with the Cleveland Report's conclusions about the reliability of children's evidence in sexual abuse cases. This caught him off his guard, but he was able to escape from the trap by 'thinking on his feet' and replying that the present case went far beyond mere sexual abuse, so the Cleveland Report's conclusions were not really relevant here. This may have been a clever answer, but it owed more to the psychiatrist's tactical and communication skills than it did to his expertise in assessing children and parents. An equally skilful psychiatrist who was less adept at thinking on his feet might have been made to appear foolish and ignorant with the result that his evidence was discounted by the judge. This may be good legal practice, but it is not a particularly good way of deciding what is best for children.

As they become more experienced in legal work, psychiatrists learn to prepare themselves for the courtroom. They try to anticipate the sort of questions they are likely to be asked in cross-examination in order to have responses ready and not be caught off their guard. They may read books and articles on court procedures and the art of giving expert evidence. They may go to the library and refresh their memory on recent research and its possible application to the case. Little of this, we should emphasise, has anything to do with the clinical judgement that the psychiatrists apply in their assessment of children and their family situations; it has everything to do with giving a good performance in the legal arena.

This is not to say that psychiatrists and other 'child welfare experts' are all equally proficient, so that one is very much as good as another. Such attributes as having considerable experience of the issue in question, familiarity with recent research, participation in case discussions with multi-disciplinary teams, their discussions with their colleagues and their undertaking of regular in-service training are important in the job of analysing problems and helping children and families overcome their distress. Those who can claim to have all these attributes are likely to be better child psychiatrists than those who have none or few of them. Yet, for reasons that we discussed in Chapter 2, this does not necessarily mean that they will come up with a prediction that will be more accurate or a recommendation to the court that will be any more likely to promote the child's welfare than less experienced or less knowledgeable colleagues. In other words, answering questions posed by court cases and predicting with precision whether children will or will not flourish if a particular course of action is taken are not part of the *clinical* work of child psychiatrists. As *clinicians*, most child psychiatrists are very wary of drawing on simple cause and effect relationships when it comes to predicting how and in what circumstances a child will flourish.

A skilful cross-examination may, of course, expose deficiencies in the clinical assessment. Important information may not have been considered by the expert witness; other information may have been inaccurate or distorted. There may be valid alternative interpretations of the parent's or child's behaviour to that offered by the psychiatrist. The problem, however, is that within the courtroom setting it is extremely difficult to separate competence from performance. A hesitant, self-critical expert witness who appears reluctant to give straight answers to the lawyer's seemingly simple questions may well have a far better grasp of the complexities of the child's emotional difficulties than a supremely confident expert who is able to parry all the lawyer's thrusts and give a clear, unequivocal account of what is good or bad for this child. Contrast, for example, the anxieties of the psychiatrist set out above, reluctant to appear in court for fear of having to make definitive statements, with the following child psychiatrist's account of a courtroom encounter:

> I was confronted with this rather overweight young barrister who thought that he was going to demolish me, and I get rather excited in court and enjoy the cut and thrust of it actually. He said, 'Couldn't it have been that this child had just been watching videos, sexual, pornography videos?' I said, 'That's sexual abuse as well.' He was completely floored by that, he wasn't ready for that at all and I said, 'In any case, for children to observe sexual experiences is not correct. Don't you close the bedroom door if you're making love to your wife?' This really put him on the spot and then he replied, 'Well as we're only just about to have a baby your question is not really appropriate' and the magistrate or the judge then told him to shut up. I was the one who could have been told to shut up but I made my point really by theatre, by actually behaving like an advocate myself and making dramatic points that sexual abuse can occur . . . I just said this child has made a statement that he's been sexually abused and I believe him.

The clinical assessment that the child had been sexually abused was successfully defended by this psychiatrist. He did so not by reference to any objective criteria by which to test whether the child's knowledge of sexual activity came from first-hand experience or from watching videos, but by skilfully avoiding that difficult issue and making it appear that the lawyer's question was foolish and ill-considered. The fact that it is often very difficult to distinguish between children's knowledge derived from doing and that obtained from watching was entirely excluded from the court's consideration.

There are some psychiatrists, however, who refuse to enter what they see as the legal world and allow their clinical judgement to be compromised by a courtroom process which they consider to be largely irrelevant to the identification of the child's needs. One such psychiatrist, for example, told how, having battled with lawyers on many occasions, he now no longer 'fights the law'.

> I tried to go into the legal domain and convince lawyers and judges that in the legal domain I was right, because there was enough evidence. And I don't do that any more. Now I will never go into the legal domain. I always say, 'Whether this is enough evidence or not is obviously up to you. I, however, I'm a clinician and on my clinical judgement . . .' And

if lawyers then try to basically push me aside, then I, with all these big nods which I do to myself (BOWS HEAD AS IF IN COURT) to disentangle myself from the legal domain and say 'Yes, in the legal domain you might be right, because you are counsel for the father you have to ask those kind of questions and obviously you would want to discredit me even at the personal level, because that's your job.' I say that freely in court.

Nevertheless, although this psychiatrist refused to enter the legal discourse or play the courtroom game, he was often obliged to go to court in order to protect the child and carry out effective treatment in sexual abuse cases. He recognised the dangers of attempting therapy where the perpetrator of the abuse was still living with the child. In cases where the abuse was denied, he needed to go to court in order to ensure that the perpetrator was kept away from the home.

I had quite a job and met with a lot of arrogance and non-understanding when I pointed out to judges . . . that if for their own legal reasons, they have to send this man home in a case where on a clinical level I as a child psychiatrist can come to no other conclusion than that sexual abuse has taken place . . . then it is most likely that this will directly lead to further crime, because the father will take it as permission to go on abusing and this will be crime-promoting crime prevention and they [the judges] will have to take responsibility for it.

Outside the courtroom

Anyone who has been involved in legal cases involving the future welfare of children will know that what happens outside the courtroom is at least as important as the hearing itself. This is true, we suspect, of all countries where the Anglo-American system of adversarial justice applies. In English courts there is a well-established ritual which precedes most child care hearings. Almost as soon as the lawyers, litigants and witnesses arrive at the court, under the lawyers' stewardship, they form themselves into separate camps. The parents, their lawyers and their witnesses cluster in one part of the corridor or waiting room, while the social workers, their lawyers and expert witnesses huddle together in another part. The senior lawyers – in English courts usually barristers – now take charge of their respective camps. No talking with 'the enemy', even if they were, until today, your patients or clients. The only permissible contact is through the medium of the lawyers.

Eventually a lawyer emerges from one of the groups and goes across to the other group. Their lawyer detaches him/herself from the cluster of anxious witnesses and litigants and the two lawyers, clutching their bundles of papers, bend towards one another in earnest conversation. Negotiations have begun. From time to time the lawyers will return to their respective groups with a progress report, an offer, a request for more information. Then back again for another encounter.

These courtroom door negotiations are essential for the efficient operation of the legal system. At their most successful they may avoid altogether any courtroom confrontation, transforming a hotly contested case into an agreed package of measures offering protection for the child and face-saving for the parents. In most cases, however, particularly those where sexual abuse is alleged, there is little room for compromise. Here the negotiations will help to identify the issues between the parties, which witnesses need to be called, whose affidavit can go in unchallenged, how long the case is likely to take.

Whether or not the children benefit from a process which is hurried, unstructured and dominated by an adversarial model, which divides people into opposing camps, is by no means certain. In some cases it can appear to help. The immediacy of the court hearing may allow the family's lawyer to bring home to the parents the 'reality' of the situation, persuading them, for example, that the evidence is so strong that they would be advised to agree to some protective measures for the child in order to avoid the risk of the judge removing the child altogether. Similarly, the social services department may be persuaded to accept something less than removal of the child because, in the lawyer's view, there is a risk that the judge may throw out the case.

One extreme example of the outcome for the child resulting from relentless pressure exerted by legal tactics, rather than any real consideration of what was best for that child, concerned a matrimonial dispute over custody. The mother had left home with her daughter to try to establish a new life for herself and her child away from her husband. The husband's reaction was to use every means possible to try to 'win back' his daughter. There were frequent court hearings. The father moved to an 'ideal' house for a child to live and found a place in a 'perfect', small, private infants' school. Episodes from the mother's past were accumulated by father and his lawyers in order to undermine her suitability to look after a young child. She had suffered a depressive episode in her adolescence; at college she had smoked cannabis; during the marriage there had been temper tantrums; after the separation, she had violated access arrangements. At the meeting outside the court-room, the mother's lawyer urged her to reconsider her position, as the father and his lawyers had amassed even more evidence with which to discredit her and undermine her parenting ability. The psychiatrist could add little to the debate except to say that the child was distressed at the conflict between the parents and would benefit from contact with both parents and less stress between them. At the last moment the mother, apparently worn down by the persistent, relentless pressure, agreed to hand over her daughter to her former husband. The case went to court as an agreed package and the issue of the child's best interests was never fully explored.

The problem with this kind of pressured decision-making is that the eventual package that is presented to the court for its approval is likely to reflect compromises between the two sides based on their lawyers' view of the evidence and judgement of what the outcome is likely to be rather than the needs of the child, as iden-tified by an impartial assessment.

Where the lawyers together determine the contentious issues that should be presented for the court to resolve, these are often not the matters relating to the child's future welfare which most concern clinical workers. There is a risk, therefore, that these pre-court negotiations may exclude important information concerning the child, simply because they do not fit lawyers' definitions of the relevant issues or what the lawyers consider to be acceptable evidence to present to the court.

On occasions, the lawyers may decide between themselves how the case should proceed without any consultation with clinic staff who have been involved with the family. In one case, for example, where the children had been left for many months in a state of uncertainty as to their future, the lawyers went into court together, leaving everyone else waiting outside. They then emerged ten minutes later to announce that the judge had agreed to adjourn the case for three months, which was the first date available which allowed sufficient time for all the evidence to be heard.

The independent expert

Some American commentators (see Further Reading) have suggested that many of the problems that we have identified concerning expert witnesses arise because these experts appear for one or other of the contesting parties. These problems, they argue, would disappear if only the inquisitorial approach of courts appointing independent experts were to be adopted. The Clinic's experience, unfortunately, does not give much support to this optimism. In England the courts from time to time order the Clinic to carry out independent assessments of children and families. Alternatively, the Official Solicitor, who acts for the child in some

High Court cases, may call in the Clinic to carry out an assessment of the child. The fact that the psychiatrists who give evidence on the results of the Clinic's assessments in such cases are independent does not protect them from the essentially adversarial nature of the proceedings.

What tends to happen is that the psychiatrist comes to be seen by the lawyers as the linchpin of the court's decision. One psychiatrist recounts that when he arrived in court it was made clear to him that everything hinged on his opinion. Before the case began, the lawyers queued up to talk to him, to find out what he was going to say, to win him over to their side. He found it very disturbing that so much power was attributed to his opinion. He also found distasteful the attempts by the lawyers to get him to talk outside the courtroom about his views on the case, 'so that they would know what questions to ask and what not to ask' in their cross-examinations.

Although independent psychiatric experts are not hired by one or other of the parties contesting what should happen to the child, they are often obliged by the adversarial nature of the setting to take sides. As soon as it is clear whose case the expert is going to support in court, alliances are formed with the expert being regarded as 'friendly' or 'hostile'. The very fact that the expert witness is seen by the judge or magistrates as non-partisan and, therefore, someone whose opinions can be relied upon raises the status and increases the power of the expert. In some cases psychiatrists from the Clinic leave the court with the uncomfortable impression that it is they, and not the judge or magistrates, who have decided the issue. This would not matter if child psychiatry were an exact science and, the psychiatrist, like the fingerprint or DNA expert, could be confident of having reached the only correct decision. Once the legal system has elevated psychiatrists to the position of independent experts, it is very difficult for the courts not to accept their view of the child's problems and recommendations for his or her future welfare. While it may be extremely flattering to be treated with reverence and have one's opinions accepted as gospel, it is also slightly worrying, particularly when one suspects that within one's own profession other equally qualified and experienced psychiatrists could well have come to a different conclusion about the child's problems and future welfare.

Lawyers

From a clinic worker's perspective lawyers have a strong and, at times, enviable part to play. They fight to win the case for their client, but at the same time seem able to cultivate the art of detachment as part of their professional equipment, describing calmly, without emotion, the most horrific details of child physical or sexual abuse. Their transient involvement with children and families, moving swiftly on from one case to another, protects them against the emotional impact of what has happened to the children and relieves them of responsibility. At times, in matrimonial cases, they have to absorb the blind hatred of one partner for another, converting raw emotion into rational argument. They become at the same time the champion of their clients and the voice of reason in their clients' disordered lives.

This ability to move out of cases once the court has finished with them, enables lawyers to distinguish their role from that of the social worker or clinic worker, whose work with the client or family does not end on the making of a care order or a decree absolute. Yet this is not the only distinguishing feature among these professions. For lawyers representing an adult client, the part they have to play in the legal process is relatively straightforward. They take their client's instructions and try to win the case. If winning is not possible, they try to secure a compromise that will best serve their client's interests.

What are their client's interests? Lawyers are entitled to assume that adults know what is best for them. They do not have to enquire beyond the client's expressed wishes. 'I want my child back' is enough. Lawyers do not have to ask 'Why?' or 'Wouldn't it be better for you not to have the burden of your child to look after?' or 'Would it not be better for the child if she remained where she is?' Any doubts that lawyers may harbour about the wisdom of their client's wishes remain secret. Lawyers may try to influence the client away from a course of action which may appear self-destructive or damaging to others, but they are under no obligation to do so. They know that if they press too hard, the client may simply pack up and look for someone else more sympathetic or less sceptical.

Where lawyers succeed in helping the client to win the case, they cannot be held responsible for any subsequent disasters that may follow – the failure of parents to cope, the renewal of abuse, the refusal of one parent to let the other see the child. As far as they are concerned the job is over. Nobody could have predicted these consequences for certain. It is not up to the lawyers to point them out and detract from their own client's case.

From the clinic worker's perspective, life for a lawyer is relatively sweet and simple. Those mental health professionals who appear regularly as witnesses in the court find remarkable the way in which lawyers manage to change alliances and allegiances. One day they are acting for an abusing parent and the next for a social services department seeking to protect a child. The whole atmosphere is rather club-like: changing partners in a tennis or bridge tournament; now you are for me, now against, but we are all members of the club, 'nothing personal in it, just doing my best, see you afterwards for a drink.' It is seductive and, in a way, fun; the clients, the cases come and go.

At least that was how it was until lawyers started to represent children's interests in civil cases. Acting for a young child causes problems. Even where the client is old enough to express his or her wishes, you cannot just accept those wishes as instructions and fight for them in court. What children want is not necessarily what is best for them. An abused or neglected child may want to remain with the parent who has caused him or her harm, despite the obvious dangers. You have to find out what is best for the child. Do the risks of letting the child stay at home outweigh those of uprooting him or her to a foster family with the subsequent risk that the fostering might break down? Who can answer such difficult questions?

Clearly, legal training does little to help lawyers find the answers. They can, of course, rely upon their background knowledge, their intuition, their personal conviction as to what is right for the child. Alternatively, they may discover the answers from the guardian *ad litem* or from the psychiatrists and psychologists who have assessed the child. Then again, they may take an agnostic approach and test out all the witnesses in court with searching questions about the likely outcomes for the child of the various courses of action proposed. Whatever line the lawyer takes, one thing is clear: this is far removed from the traditional lawyer–client relationship. Instead of being an advocate for the client's wishes, the lawyer becomes an advocate for the client's *welfare* – a temporary trustee for the child.

This trustee role has led to the emergence of a new breed of lawyer, one who is removed from the courtroom fray between family and social services department or between warring parents; one whose job it is to press for the child's rights to be respected and the child's interests promoted. It is a role which it is difficult to fulfil, even temporarily, without some emotional involvement. When lawyers who have represented children in abuse or neglect cases next act for a parent, they tend to be much more circumspect about fighting to win the case, regardless of the effects on the child. Many are reluctant to accept the parent's wishes, right or wrong. They may try to persuade the parents to accept a compromise which offers some protection to the child or which acknowledges implicitly the deficiencies of the parent(s).

In child care cases some lawyers are attempting to counsel parents to consider the best interest of their children and try to arrive at an agreement with social services. In divorce cases some lawyers prefer to take on a conciliatory role, often because they believe that conciliation is a better way of dealing with disputes over the children than fighting every inch of the way, using the children as ammunition in the matrimonial battle. Some jurisdictions have included obligatory conciliation as part of the divorcing process. These changes may be helpful to the children and may reduce the adversarial nature of hearings, but problems still remain.

Research in the USA (see Further Reading) has shown how some lawyers will exploit conciliation in order to gain advantages for their client. For them winning the case and not promoting children's interests is still the overriding objective. The lawyer who takes a child-orientated view then finds himself out-manoeuvred by his 'opponents'. The client is furious at losing the case or being forced to accept an unsatisfactory deal out of court. The lawyer realises that child-orientated law only works if all lawyers are playing the same game.

In child care proceedings what happens to parents who refuse to be persuaded by professional advice and who want to continue the fight for their child? Should not lawyers be obliged to represent the parents' wishes, to fight for parental rights, although they realise that the child might become the innocent victim of any prolonged and bitter legal wrangle? Once they have given up their original role, lawyers risk becoming amateur social workers. Yet they can never fully abandon their traditional role. For lawyers to accept, for example, that the legal process itself may be harmful for children, and that some extra-legal method might be preferable for dealing with disputes between state and parent or between parents over the protection and welfare of children, would be to deprive themselves of a role, status, business. The tendency rather is to call for reforms of the system such as video evidence, psychological experts or training programmes for lawyers and judges which, far from removing the delicate and complex cases involving children's welfare to a more appropriate setting than courts of law, retain and increase the lawyer's role, albeit in a form which gives the impression that lawyers are moving with the times and are well able to cope with the new demands made of them.

Summing up

1. We began this chapter with an account of a psychiatrist's visit to an English juvenile court to give expert evidence in a child care case. She described her disgust at the appalling lack of facilities and the Dickensian atmosphere with parents in child care cases being forced to share a waiting area with drunks and violent petty criminals. We pointed out how the physical environment of the court can influence the attitudes of the participants and the nature of the courtroom hearing.

2. Several psychiatrists recalled their experience in giving expert evidence in court. A common response was for the first occasion to be a major ordeal but, after a few times, knowing what to expect, the psychiatrists found that things became much easier. Some even seem to relish the opportunity to go to court and do battle 'in public' with the lawyers and rival experts. Others still feel uncomfortable about having their opinions forced into a legal framework. We pointed out what we saw as the dangers of socialising child psychiatrists into the legal process.

3. We then examined the belief that the cross-examination of psychiatric experts in court in some way makes them accountable to the public. Our view is that the object of courtroom cross-examination is to undermine and cast doubt upon the credibility of experts by exposing weaknesses in their opinions and the procedures by which they reached those opinions. It is the psychiatrists' ability to defend their views which is examined, not how good they are at their job. More importantly, courtroom contests between lawyer and expert, or between two experts with opposing views, may expose the state of the art in assessment of parenting and prediction of outcomes, but they do not go very far towards finding ways to serve the child's best interests.

4. While supporting in general terms the use of an independent expert to advise the court, we are aware that this vests enormous power in the hands of one person. We deplore the spectacle that occurs on occasion in English courts of lawyers for rival parties competing to gain the vote of the expert for their client. Once again, we wonder whose interests are being served by this spectacle.

5. We considered the detached way in which lawyers are able to operate and its advantages in cases which are emotionally highly charged. Such detachment absolves them from any responsibility for the effects on the child of the outcome of the case. In particular it relieves them from having to confront the moral dilemma of acting for a client who is determined to pursue a course of action which may well be detrimental to the child's welfare. We

questioned whether this ability to remain detached was weakened when lawyers came to represent the interest of the child in court. Here, we suggested, the lawyer becomes a temporary trustee of the child's welfare.

Discussion

Our criticisms of the courts and the legal process in this and previous chapters clearly indicate that much could be done to improve the quality of justice for those children and parents who become immersed in legal proceedings. We would put high on our list of priorities the improvement of court facilities, some lessening of the ordeal-like nature of court hearings and the education of judges, magistrates and lawyers in basic principles of child care and development. However, we do not wish to give the impression that once these improvements had been achieved all would be well. Far from it. For most of the time the law is an inappropriate institution for determining child welfare issues. Furthermore, attempts to improve the legal system by importing experts from outside may paradoxically make matters worse by giving the impression that specialist family courts or children's courts now have the capability for resolving difficult problems. The danger is that when parents, social workers and even workers at child mental health clinics simply do not know what to do, they will tell themselves that the only way out is to 'let the court decide'. Our argument is that the only way the courts can decide complex issues is by reducing them to simple ones and, in doing so, much that concerns the child's future welfare disappears from view. No amount of education for lawyers, judges and magistrates, or of improvements to make the courts more informal, more customer-friendly, is going to change this, for its roots lie deep in the social functions that the legal system fulfils.

For evidence of this argument one need look no further than the United States, where many of the reforms that have been proposed in the United Kingdom have already been carried out. Yet it is still possible for children like Hilary – whose mother Elizabeth Morgan was jailed in America for refusing to disclose her daughter's whereabouts to the court in order to protect her from the possibility of sexual abuse from the child's father (see Further Reading) – to be torn apart by a system which is more concerned with establishing something called 'the truth' and providing justice for warring parents than with promoting children's welfare.

Further reading

Child mental health professionals in court

'Children and the Legal Process: Views from a Mental Health Clinic' by Michael King, *Journal of Social Welfare and Family Law* (1991) no. 4, pp. 269–84.

The Evidence of Children: The Law and the Psychology by J.R. Spencer and Rhona Flin, ch. 9 (Blackstone Press, 1990).

Hilary's Trial: The Elizabeth Morgan Case – A Child's Ordeal in the American Legal System by Jonathan Groner (Simon and Schuster, 1991).

How the Law Thinks about Children by Michael King and Christine Piper (Gower, 1990).

The Multi-professional Handbook of Child Sexual Abuse: Integrated Management, Therapy and Legal Intervention by Tilman Furniss, ch. 5 (Routledge, 1991).

Lawyers in child welfare and custody disputes and in the conciliation process

Hilary's Trial (as above).

'The Impact of Divorce Mediation on Legal Practice in Maine' by C. McEwen, R. Mainman and L. Mather. Paper presented at the Conference of the Socio-Legal Association, Bristol, April 1990.

'Law and Strategy in the Divorce Lawyer's Office' by A. Sarat and W. Felstiner, *Law and Society Review* (1986) 21, no. 1, p. 93.

'Participation and Flexibility in Informal Processes: Cautions from the Divorce Court Context' by H. Ehrlanger and others, *Law and Society Review* (1986) 21, no. 4, pp. 585–604.

Partisans and Mediators: The Resolution of Divorce Disputes by Gwynn Davis (Clarendon Press, 1988).

Proposal for court-appointed expert

'Child Sexual Abuse: Re-establishing the Balance within the Adversary System' by Mary Hutton, *Michigan Journal of Law Reform* (1987) 20, p. 491.

'Issues in Civil Procedure' by E. Donald Elliott, *Boston University Law Review* (1989) 69, p. 487.

7

Responding to Children's Needs:
an Issue of Law?

The time has come to pull together some of the threads that we have left trailing behind us in earlier chapters. We start with the main subject of this book: the effects of the law and the operation of the legal system upon those children and families who become the subject of legal proceedings.

The impression of the law that may have been gained by the cases that we have presented could well be that of a largely inflexible and insensitive institution which inflicts its rules and decisions upon families, social workers and psychiatrists alike. At times, the outcome of legal cases may appear to have scant regard for the well-being of the children whose interests the law is trying to promote and at other times they may be based on a simplistic, rudimentary understanding of child psychology and, in particular, of the world as it appears to young children. Moreover, confrontations within the law appear to many non-lawyers who become involved in child care cases as rather unpleasant and best avoided wherever possible. If they are unavoidable, then you have to play the game according to the arcane and artificial legal rules.

Yet, at the same time, there exists among most social workers and mental health workers a respect for the courts as necessary and important for the protection of people's rights and, along side this respect, the hope, perhaps against all the odds, that some way out of the confusion over the child's future will emerge from the legal proceedings. The hope also abounds that things will get better, when judges and lawyers are more specialised and trained in child care, when the rules of evidence are changed and, of course, when family courts arrive.

Yet much of these criticisms and hopes for change arise from expectations of the legal system which it can never realistically meet, given the inherent nature of law as a social institution. Only by ceasing to produce legal decisions can the legal system take on the role of therapist and promoter of children's interests. If we are to understand the limits of what law can do and what the legal system can become, we need to examine the functions that law performs in modern societies and then go on to see whether, or to what extent, these functions are compatible with the sensitive, child-responsive legal system that many who work in the child care field want to exist.

Law's social functions

1. Maintaining social cohesion

Issues concerning child welfare and child protection presented by legal textbooks and by the reports of court cases tend to be simplified, sanitised accounts of reality as it is perceived from mental health clinics. Much of the complexity of interwoven emotional relationships is reduced and simplified by the legal process to dimensions that can be made to fit pre-existing legal categories. This process, far from reflecting inadequacies in the legal system that can be remedied by improvements in procedures and the quality of legal representation, is an essential part of the law's social role. Law, according to recent theoretical ideas about the nature of law as a social institution, needs to convey simple, straightforward moral messages to the external world. It does so in part by ignoring or simplifying just those complexities and ambivalences in human relationships that clinical workers thrive upon.

Just as in fairy stories the characters tend to be one-dimensional cardboard cut-outs, symbolising different moral positions – the good fairy, the wicked fairy, the evil giant, the protective dwarfs etc. – so in legal stories real-life characters tend to be portrayed as caricatures. Moreover, as in fairy stories, legal stories contain a coded message or moral concealed in the narrative. The law's messages may be concerned with simple moral issues demonstrating, for example, how 'bad' parents lose their children or how 'innocent children' are protected against evil. However, the message is equally likely to celebrate the just nature of law itself. The law, for example is fair because it protects the weak, rewards virtue and innocence, punishes the guilty and seeks out where children's best interests lie.

This does not mean to say that all legal decisions are perfect. Law, like life, is imperfect – judges may from time to time criticise past legal decisions – but it is always presented as striving to improve its performance. Judges who fifty years ago may have minimised the effects of separating a young child from its mother are seen by today's judges as having been misguided. But today's judges are perceived as being 'correct' in maintaining that living with both parents is best for the healthy development of the child (except, of course, where one of the parents has sexually abused the child, in which case the parent is seen as 'evil' and generally denied contact with his children).

This, then, is not just a matter of judges keeping abreast of current knowledge about what is good and bad for children. Such knowledge is rather digested by the legal system and emerges as legal principles, overlaid with strong moral messages which serve to educate both litigants and people in general about what is and what is not acceptable behaviour in relations between parents and among parents, social workers and children. These legal stories present a seemingly consensual view about children's needs and ways of meeting those needs through good practice and good parenting. The fact that in the external, non-legal world such a consensus does not exist has to be ignored in legal stories. For the law to enter into the controversies over psychological theory and the validity or otherwise of research studies would be both to generate uncertainty among parents, social workers and other care takers and to undermine confidence in the law itself (as well as in psychological expertise) and its ability to resolve disputes in a just manner.

2. Promoting 'the public interest'

The degree to which the legal system has a responsibility for maintaining social order and promoting the public interest over and above its responsibility towards the parties to a legal dispute is a matter of much discussion among lawyers. In practice, the public interest as interpreted by the judges tends to prevail over the private interests of litigants, witnesses etc. This, however, can conflict with the legal principle that children's welfare shall be paramount.

There are not many people who would be prepared to dispute that a young child of, say, six years, who had been the only witness to a murder, should wherever possible give evidence regardless of any possible trauma that could be caused by the child reliving his or her experience in court and being subjected to cross-examination. A balance has to be made between the harm likely to be caused to the child and the interests of law and order, of public safety. Where the crime is child sexual abuse and the suspected perpetrator is a stranger who is suspected by the police of having carried out several minor sexual assaults on different children, the same balancing exercise applies, only this time it may well be that the harm to the child in appearing as a witness outweighs the benefit to society from prosecuting the abuser. Let us change the facts slightly and make the perpetrator the child's father, and the abuse more serious. Does public interest now demand that the child give evidence, regardless of the likely harm that will be caused to the child?

Although we have deliberately avoided discussing criminal prosecutions, this does not entitle us to avoid difficult questions about how far the traditional (and, some would say, essential) roles of the law in our society should be curtailed by considerations about the effects on children's welfare. Our position is that where there is a serious risk of harm to the child through the use of the legal process, everything possible should be done to minimise that risk. This would involve not only such measures as video-links and the admissibility of previously recorded video evidence (Piggot Committee Report), but also a greater sensitivity to children's needs throughout the criminal justice system.

3. Conflict management

Where a couple are locked in battle over who should have the care of the children, are they not entitled to turn to the law, as the social institution charged with conflict resolution, and demand a determination of their dispute? Is not the law required to give that decision quite regardless either of the effects of the legal process upon the children or of the possibility that a cut-and-dried decision giving one parent custody may result in the loss for the children of all contact with the other parent?

In child abuse and neglect cases, is it not up to state agencies who wish to intervene in family life to prove in law that abuse has occurred and that action by the state is justified and necessary for the children's protection? If the law were to abdicate its responsibility, would this not leave the way open for tyranny by experts, with paediatricians, child psychiatrists and social workers taking it upon themselves to remove children from parents whenever they pleased?

These are difficult policy issues. Clearly, there needs to be some control over the power of experts and the representatives of state agencies. This control may well take the form of legislation laying down strict limits for coercive intervention to protect children. This begs the question, however, over the distinction between persuasion and coercion. What Anglo-American systems have tended to do is to lay the emphasis upon the integrity of the family unit and to treat any threat to that integrity as potentially a matter of conflict for the courts to adjudicate upon. What several European countries, notably France, Belgium and Holland, have done by contrast is to use the persuasive powers of officialdom so that the incidence of naked coercion is minimal and the number of cases requiring adjudication of a legal nature very small indeed.

The issue that concerns us here is not which of these approaches is fairer or more democratic, but which one is likely to cause the least harm to the children that the state is trying to protect. To insist as a matter of principle upon the legal adjudication through a full-blown courtroom contest of every matter where the state's representatives seek to protect children in ways which conflict with the parents makes little sense, if attempts to put the principle into practice actually hurt the vulnerable individuals that the law is trying to protect. What we would argue is that, in the understandable quest of lawyers, administrators and politicians in Anglo-Saxon countries for a just and fair system, the harm caused to the relationships between parents and children and between families and their social worker or clinic is all too often ignored.

The other area of conflict which regularly finds expression in the courts involves parental disputes over children. Here again, on the strength of the case histories that we have presented, we would question the use of the law, particularly as it operates in Anglo-American systems, as necessarily the appropriate institution for managing conflicts of this kind. The problem with the systematic use of the legal process lies in its method of conflict management. By structuring as a legal contest the emotional tangle that often follows the break-up of close relationships, the law may succeed in channelling and so managing the conflict. In doing so, however, it allows the hostility and acrimony to find expression and feed upon the many opportunities that the legal process itself offers for humiliating, outwitting and defeating the once-loved-and-now-despised former partner or the once-helpful-and-now-interfering social worker. In this paradox of conflict management, through the ritualised expression of conflict, it is the child once again who is likely to suffer, pulled in different directions by opposing parties.

Recent changes in the substantive law, such as the English Children Act, remove the obligation for parents to seek a court order for the children solely because they are divorcing. Nevertheless, whenever there is disagreement between them over the residence and visiting arrangements, the image of the child in a *Caucasian Chalk Circle*, on the point of being torn apart by rival carers intent on winning their claim to have the child living with them, has not been dispelled by the implementation in England and Wales of the Children Act 1989 or by the arrival in other countries of family courts.

Once again, from the child welfare perspective, persuasion is almost always better than coercion. The best conciliation services are able to offer education for parents on the deleterious effects on their children of unrestrained hostility and in doing so avoid the need to seek out a legal resolution of their conflict. However, other forms of conciliation may simply pressure parents into accepting compromises as an alternative to expensive and risky litigation. There may be agreement on paper, but no real commitment to work together for the sake of the children.

4. The protection of rights

There are important issues to be raised concerning the courts' role as protector of rights. In the first place we need to consider the concept of legal rights by dividing them into two, *substantive rights* and *procedural rights*. Substantive rights provide the rights-holder, whether a parent, child or organisation such as the family or social services, with the power, enforceable by law, to take action affecting others or to resist action taken by others against that individual or organisation. Procedural rights, on the other hand, exist only to ensure fairness during the process of decision-making, whether in a court or elsewhere. Unlike substantive rights, they do not determine the outcome of the decision, but only the form of the decision-making process.

Substantive rights: The legal process works relatively well as a protector of substantive rights when it is asked to rule upon issues arising out of a contractual arrangement, such as landlord and tenant or seller and buyer. It may also work well when faced with such quasi-contractual situations as teacher–pupil or trustee–beneficiary. However, it works far less well for those relationships which are based upon a complex interweaving of emotional and economic factors such as one finds in family issues. While it may be able to regulate the economic relationship by deciding, for example, that the couple should share equally the proceeds of sale of the matrimonial home, it often has to leave emotional conflicts to be resolved outside the courtroom. In child protection cases, however, it is often not possible for law to renounce responsibility in the fraught area of emotions. To reduce the complexities to issues of rights and their infringement may be the only way that the legal process can give the impression of dealing effectively with such conflicts. The suspicion remains, however, that the rights rhetoric is covering up vast areas of human experience which law is ill equipped to tackle.

The recent Children Act for England and Wales deliberately avoids the use of the term 'rights' in relation to children, their families and state agencies, preferring instead concepts such as parental 'duties' and 'responsibilities', children's needs and welfare. Despite this change in the terminology, the Act still gives social services departments the power to remove children from their parents where this is necessary for the child's protection. It gives parents the (procedural) legal right to challenge these decisions in court and it asks the court to make a wide range of decisions where the rights of parents and families to self-determination have to be balanced against the rights of children to protection from harm. Furthermore, the courts, under the provisions of the Act, are still engaged in binary (right/wrong) decisions where parents attempt to protect their rights by denying that their child is in danger of significant harm and the social services department try to show that the child is indeed in danger of such harm and by doing so to secure through a court order the right of the child to protection. Although the terms may have changed, the essentials of the process remain largely unaltered whereby the complexities of intra-family relations continue to be simplified and reduced to issues that can be handled effectively by court procedures and decisions and by the intermittent nature of the court's involvement in the child's welfare. The change of vocabulary, then, does not in practice give rise to a change of substance in the kinds of decisions that courts are required to make.

This Act, like many other statutes existing in different countries, gives substantive rights to families to be free from interference by state agencies, as long as the children are not abused or in danger of harm. It also gives procedural rights to both parents and children. Few people would argue with the need to restrain agencies from the arbitrary use of state power or with the objective of protecting children. Yet the very fact that issues concerning children's welfare are, as we have shown, defined as a conflict between state and parents which only the courts can resolve, raises serious questions over whose interests are in fact being served by this use of the legal process. Similarly, nobody would deny that procedural rights for parents and children are important, but they do not mean that every disagreement between parents and social services departments should provide the opportunity for a full-blooded court trial with lawyers representing all the various parties who may have an interest in the child's future. These matters become clearer if we examine how the substantive and procedural rights of children operate in practice.

In essence, children's substantive rights may be summarised as (a) the right to be free from any conduct or situation likely to cause them harm and (b) the right of self-determination or autonomy – the power to make choices about their own lives. We have already seen how the enforcement of the first of these substantive rights will often be outside the powers of any court, depending instead on the availability of resources to meet the child's needs. Where the courts become involved, therefore, the issues are likely to be confined to harm caused by the parents or other adult care-takers. Courts may deal with harm caused by individuals, but they are relatively powerless when it comes to harm resulting from government policies or poor administration.

A similar problem arises in relation to the child's right to make choices. The child's choices will depend upon what is available. In the famous English case of *Gillick* ([1985] 2WLR, 830, House of Lords), for example, the children's right to contraception and contraceptive advice, won through the courts, would be meaningless if there were no clinics available to offer this service to teenagers or if the only clinics offering the service charged fees which were far beyond what the Gillick children could afford. Similarly, a child in the care of a social services department cannot choose to be placed in a children's home rather than a foster family if the local council for the area closed all children's homes as an economy measure some five years previously.

A second problem for the promoters of children's autonomous rights through legal intervention is that what the child wants may not coincide with what the law wants. Parents may be prosecuted and imprisoned for child abuse without any consultation with the children, and the children may be removed from the home 'for their own safety', regardless of their wishes and at times without any attempt to find out their wishes. Where these matters are discussed with children, it is difficult to know how much influence on the course of events they have or should have and how much should be determined by the professionals involved.

Older children may be in a position to exercise some influence over the legal process, but it takes considerable courage and perseverance on the child's part to resist the relentless pressure from the legal machine. Take the example of a fifteen-year-old girl who had told a local authority social worker that her step-father had been sexually abusing her. She made it clear that, while she wanted the abuse to stop, she wished to remain at home and that she would refuse to repeat her allegations to the police or in court. The social services decided that, since she was old enough and sufficiently mature to have the right to make decisions for herself, they would offer her hostel accommodation and would not take legal proceedings. In this case it was paradoxically only by keeping the issue out of the legal arena that the substantive rights of the child could be protected.

A final problem can arise when children's rights are rigidly promoted and thus may actually cause harm to the children. An illustration comes from the case of an eleven-year-old girl who had been placed in a foster home after her mother, who was suffering from a psychotic illness, had failed to seek medical treatment when the child was dangerously ill. When she was interviewed at the

Clinic the girl said that she wanted to return home, but at the same interview recalled how unhappy she had been living with her mother. Her drawings and play confirmed the ambivalence of the relationship with the mother and the child's anxieties about returning to live with her. While living in foster care her physical health and school performance had improved considerably. The mother, on the other hand, continued to suffer from psychotic episodes. If the law had given this child a substantive right of self-determination, a court would have had no option but to return the child home – a result that would in all probability have increased the child's suffering and the risk of long-term damage.

A law which gives children the right to choose imposes a burden of responsibility which many children, even some of those who have reached adolescence, are not ready to bear. For children to have to decide which parent they wish to live with after a divorce would in many cases cause severe conflicts of loyalty and feelings of guilt towards the 'deserted' parent. Perhaps, if children are to be given any substantive rights in this situation, it should be the right not to have responsibility for their parents thrust upon them.

Our concerns over the use of the courts and legal system to protect children's substantive rights may be summarised in the following way:

(a) The rights of children are not necessarily the same as the needs of children.

(b) In many instances the courts are unable to protect children's rights because they have no control over the resources on which those rights depend.

(c) In some cases the use of the legal system to force others to take account of children's rights may cause the child more harm than leaving matters as they are.

Procedural rights　These are rights which guarantee that children will be treated fairly in the decision-making process, but which do not in themselves directly affect decisions. They include the right to express an opinion on any matter which concerns their future welfare. In formal decision-making processes, such as courts and case conferences, they may require an adult (not necessarily a lawyer) to represent the child.

The concept of procedural rights may extend to any situation where adults have power over children's lives, such as schools, children's homes and foster homes, and may require some complaints procedure to enable the child's grievances to be heard. Whether or not the existence of a complaints procedure should be extended to children in their own families is a controversial issue.

In Sweden the Children's Ombudsman is available to listen to such complaints (see Chapter 8, Further Reading), and in France any child is entitled to write to the children's judge requesting an audience. These procedures are particularly valuable for older children whose parents will not grant them the freedoms that they feel are appropriate for their age. In most Anglo-Saxon countries, however, the only way in which children may challenge parental decisions is through the courts and even then they have to find a sympathetic adult to bring the case on their behalf.

It would be wrong to underestimate the importance of these procedural rights for children in influencing social attitudes towards children and the importance of the law in ensuring that these rights are respected. However, this is not the same thing as using the courts and the whole paraphernalia of the legal process each time that an important decision has to be made concerning the child's welfare or on each occasion that a child has a grievance to be aired. There is a world of difference between using the formal legal process to ensure that decisions about children are made according to procedures that are fair and just to the child and using that process regularly to determine what course of action would best promote the child's welfare or best interests.

The fact that some countries, such as France and Sweden, may appear to use their courts successfully to make substantive, welfare decisions about children may seem to contradict this distinction between the substantive and the procedural. However, if one examines more closely the actual decision-making process, one finds that the specialised procedures for child welfare decisions in these countries' courts are both informal and conciliatory in their approach (see Chapter 8). They tend to be much closer to mediation sessions than to courtroom trials.

5. Establishing the facts

Many disputes that are brought to the legal system for resolution do not involve arguments about what the law says, but revolve rather around arguments over what happened. Much of the legal process, therefore, is concerned with discovering 'the truth' about past events. Were promises made? Was the car going too fast? Were any blows struck? Did the newspaper article lie about the private life of some celebrity? The legal system, therefore, holds itself out to be not just a resource for determining disputes about the interpretation of laws, but also an institution where 'the truth' can be established. The law provides in the courts a forum for establishing the truth where rules governing procedure, standards of proof and admissibility of evidence ensure consistency and fairness. In Anglo-American systems these rules are strict and rigid in criminal trials, but in civil cases there is a growing tendency for the rules to be relaxed or dispensed with altogether.

This does not mean, however, that civil proceedings have ceased to be adversarial, but rather that there is much more scope than in criminal cases for the parties to negotiate between themselves as to what facts should be admitted without formal proof and what form the proof should take. Nor does it mean that civil proceedings, including child protection cases or parental disputes over children, are any less determinants of right and wrong. It is rare for these cases not to involve some argument over past events. Child protection case issues often revolve around the answers to these questions: 'Was the injury caused by the abuse?' 'Who was responsible for the abuse?' 'Who could have prevented it?' In inter-parental disputes there are different issues. 'Has the parent been loving, caring, responsible?' Courts will be asked to decide whose version of 'the truth' should prevail.

Establishing 'the facts' is not only a matter of courts finding cases proved or unproved or deciding for one party in preference to the other. In their decisions on the facts the courts in the Anglo-American system convey important messages to children and parents and to all those involved with the family. Even where court hearings take place in private in the absence of the press, all those concerned in the proceedings treat court decisions as authoritative statements of right and wrong, true and false.

This may be particularly important in those cases where the child has accused an adult of abuse. The official recognition of the fact that the child's allegations were well-founded may provide the child and those agencies trying to help the family with a solid foundation for their work. In the case of successful criminal prosecutions, the legal label in the form of a criminal record which is attached to the child abuser may in the future help to save other children from abuse.

However, there is a down side to the Anglo-American preoccupation with establishing 'the facts' in court. When the court fails to confirm the child's version of events, the result is often seen as a vindication of the alleged perpetrator. The implicit message that may emerge from the court is that the child should not be believed. Yet, as we have explained, the court's decision may be influenced by a number of different factors, including the inadmissibility of crucial evidence, the performance of witnesses in court and the selective perceptions of judges, magistrates or juries. What the court decides to be 'the facts' may not, therefore, correspond with 'the truth' as recognised by others whose knowledge of the child and family is not confined by artificial rules or restricted to snap-shot exposures. This version of the truth may see the child's allegations as well-founded and the court's refusal to accept them as an encouragement to the perpetrator to repeat the abuse.

Let us turn now from the functions of the law to examine to what extent these functions are compatible with the process of identifying and promoting children's needs.

Children's needs and the law

References to children's needs, the welfare of children, the child's best interests have proliferated in the statutes and law reports of all those countries where the Anglo-American system of justice applies. Some jurisdictions go as far as to list in detail the needs of children, while others leave matters very much to the interpretation of the courts in individual cases. The cumulative impression that they give is that the legal system is capable not only of resolving disputes between state and family, or between parents, or between parents and other child-carers but also of bringing the knowledge and wisdom of the law to bear upon complex issues concerning children's needs and even of promoting the needs of individual children.

We have little doubt that many judges, magistrates and lawyers believe this to be true and that this belief acts as a strong motivation for their involvement in the emotionally draining work of the family courts. Yet, there is also a danger that lawyers, judges, magistrates and others with a vested interest in keeping things much as they are at present, will tend to exaggerate the uniqueness and exclusiveness of the law's traditional roles and overemphasise the benefits to be gained through legal decisions and the legal process through such devices as the protection of individual rights, both procedural and substantive.

The criticisms that we have made concerning the use of legal intervention in child welfare cases are unlikely to please them. Nor are they likely to please those politicians who for ideological or economic reasons tend to see the passing of laws as an end in itself, with little concern to understand the limitations and dynamics of those institutions charged with putting laws into effect.

While we accept without any hesitation that, as individuals, sympathetic and well-intentioned lawyers and judges may from time to time be able to improve the lives of children whose problems come before the courts, this is not, we would argue, because they are lawyers and judges, but because they are sympathetic and concerned individuals. By forcing good intentions to

conform to very precise and correct forms (in order to protect
rights and prevent the arbitrary use of power), the legal process
may at times actually inhibit these good intentions or hem them in
with conditions and provisos which detract from their benevolence.
Nor should it be thought that tinkering with that process will in
itself bring about changes in the fundamental nature of law and the
social functions that the legal system serves. The legal process is
not, for example, going to provide those material and emotional
resources that give children security and allow them to blossom.
Generally, all that law can do effectively is to manage the conflicts
that arise between adults over the extent and nature of their relationships with children. Even here one may well question how
effective the law is as a social institution for conflict management
where the subject of the conflicts consists, not of material goods
or property, but of relationships and emotional engagements.

Yet to leave these difficult emotional conflicts festering and
unresolved may result in ambivalence and uncertainty in people's
relationships with one another and to the children who are dependent on them. People may be reluctant to commit themselves to
situations or relationships where their rights and responsibilities are
unclear, where they cannot predict what the outcome will be if
things go wrong. The most that can be said of law as a social
institution performing essentially legal functions, as opposed to
well-meaning judges and lawyers as individuals, is that it may on
occasion help to influence adult's behaviour towards children in
positive ways, but it is only one factor among many and often not
a very important factor at that.

There is, unfortunately, the negative side of law to be taken into
account. As we have seen, the operation of the legal process in
children's cases may create more problems than it solves. Conflicts
tend to be heightened; people tend to become more entrenched in
their positions, rejecting any compromise as a loss of face and any
concession as a defeat for their cause. Yet what appears like a
major success for the lawyers in persuading the parties to a dispute
to give up their excessive demands and recognise the importance of
their children's welfare may, on closer examination, reveal itself as
something less than a triumph for law. With adequate preventive
measures and the availability of alternative, non-adversarial
processes for resolving disputes, the conflict might never have
reached such proportions. In other words, the legal process might
in some (but not all) cases be doing no more than dealing with the
problems that it itself has in part created.

Unfortunately, we can offer no magic remedy to these problems
or dramatic revelations which are going to revolutionise child care

or the legal system. Instead, we take a step backwards in two distinct senses. First, we go back to reconsider four case histories which we presented in earlier chapters. Secondly, we take a step backwards – to distance ourselves from the detailed problems of specific child-care and legal systems. From this detached vantage point we apply to these cases certain principles, derived from our previous discussions, which we believe to be important in promoting children's well-being. These principles relate to early preventive intervention, working with families to protect children and promote their welfare. They also concern limits to the effective use of the legal system and the potential harm to the child and family if these limits are infringed.

Each of the four cases that we have chosen for this detailed analysis presents different problems and calls out for different types of solution. The first concerns the 'yo-yo' child whose case is described in Chapter 3. The problem here was one of how to handle a parent–child relationship where a single parent suffered from recurrent bouts of serious mental illness. The second case involves a young child, whose parents were in the throes of a matrimonial dispute, telling her mother that her father had sexually abused her during access visits (Chapter 4). Next, we reconsider the plight of the young couple whose housing and financial problems combined with the stress of caring for difficult young children led to abuse (Chapter 2). Sexual abuse by a father is also at the centre of our fourth case (Chapter 5). Here, the parents had separated some years previously and the allegations of abuse were of a much more serious nature.

Case 1 (Chapter 3, pp. 49–50)

This was the case of a six-year-old boy with a young mother who suffered from a manic-depressive illness. The child's parents had met while both of them were undergoing treatment at a psychiatric hospital. On discharge from hospital, they had lived together in a pleasant council flat and it was during this period that their son was conceived. The birth and the baby's early weeks went smoothly enough, the couple receiving considerable support during this period from health and social services. As the baby grew and the support tailed off, however, the father found the demands made by a small child increasingly difficult. When the baby was nine months old, he left forever.

The mother felt abandoned both by her man and by the health and welfare services which had supported her so well during the early stages of the child's development. There followed repeated episodes of depression which resulted in her being admitted to hospital on several occasions. Each time the child was placed with a short-term foster family under a voluntary care agreement. After six such placements, the local authority decided to apply to court for a care order so that permanent arrangements could be made for the care of the child. The mother resisted the application. The magistrates refused the request for a care order, believing that a supervision order would be sufficient to protect the child. A second application to change the supervision order into a care order, when the mother had once again been admitted to hospital, was also turned down. However, when, after thirteen hospital admissions and periods of short-term fostering, the case came back to court for a third time, with an assessment from a psychiatrist from the Clinic that the child was suffering from these constant switches of home and care-taker, the court decided that a care order was the only answer. The child was placed immediately with long-term foster parents who were unwilling for the mother to maintain regular contact with her son until he had established a firm relationship with his 'new family'.

What could have been done?

First, there could have been much more support for the young couple early on, before the father left. With the benefit of hindsight, it is clear that two very young parents with a history of mental illness were extremely vulnerable. Was there no possibility at that stage, for example, of the whole family being admitted to a residential young family unit where they could have received help and guidance on how to care for their baby? If the risks of the relationship breaking down had been recognised early on, the family might have remained intact. If this had happened, some support from within the family might have been available during the mother's depressive bouts, so avoiding hospital admission and separation from her child.

Secondly, after the father had walked out, should not the young child have accompanied his mother to hospital instead of being put into care? Mother and baby units did exist in psychiatric hospitals at that time, but they were rapidly being closed down as a result of health service cuts and a national policy of care in the community for mental patients. If it had been possible to deal with the problem in this way, any transition to substitute care might have been much easier. Where the hospital staff had seen mother and child interacting over a long period, either clear indications might have become apparent that the relationship between mother and child was sufficiently good to warrant doing everything possible to provide support for the mother or there might have been an irrefutable case for concluding that the mother was quite unable to cope. In this case the staff might have been able to persuade her to have the child placed in long-term fostering without the need for three court applications and three contested care hearings.

Thirdly, even if this young mother had persistently refused to part with her child, it might still have been possible to avoid full-blown courtroom contests, the removal of parental rights and the ending of parental visits. If there had existed some informal process (as in France or Holland) presided over by someone independent of the professional workers involved in the case, charged with attempting to secure parental agreement for measures to further the child's interests, it is possible that some arrangement could have been mutually accepted whereby the child would be placed with a long-term foster family, but the mother should have regular access. Of course, such an arrangement would have had to be carefully monitored and any problems referred back to the informal hearing or tribunal. There would have been no need for any formal court hearing unless the mother wished to appeal against the decisions of the informal hearing.

Case 2 (Chapter 4, pp. 62–4)

The bitter breakdown of a young couple's marriage formed the backdrop to this allegation by a four-year-old girl that her father had 'fondled her private parts'. This marriage breakdown had occurred over a year before the incident. It had been particularly painful because both parents had been involved in looking after the little girl and both were reluctant to 'give her up'. Their short marriage had been fraught with financial and housing problems. The stress these caused, together with those of meeting the needs and demands of a baby and then a toddler, with very little support either from their respective families or from the local community, in the end had overwhelmed them. They were in their twenties and were lacking in experience and insight into how to deal with relationship problems. They ended up by blaming each other for everything that had gone wrong.

Given this bitterness, it was perhaps not surprising that as soon as she heard about the 'fondling' the mother seized the opportunity to end all contact between her daughter and her former husband. She wanted him out of their life. Nor was it surprising that he should invoke the wardship procedure in order to bring the issue before the court. He thought she was an unfit mother and wanted to have his daughter living with him.

The 'fusional' relationship between mother and daughter made it impossible to untangle the truth about the fondling. It may have been true, but the child said many vicious things about her father. Even if she had not been rehearsed by her mother, it could well have been that she had been rewarded, consciously or unconsciously, for each verbal attack on her father.

What could have been done?

By the time the case came to court the warfare between the parents had reached such a pitch that it would have been very difficult to construct a truce which would have had any lasting effect. Any effective intervention would have had to have taken place well before the court case. Yet, how far back do you go? If the mother had not had such a deprived and unhappy childhood she might well have been more stable and better equipped to deal with the demands of a close relationship, a young child and economic hardship. However, taking the early days of the marriage as the starting point, decent housing conditions and some support with the care of the child might have reduced some of the stress. But what specific kinds of intervention might have avoided the bitter separation, unhealthy relationship between mother and daughter, the allegation of sexual abuse, whether true or false, and the inconclusive court hearing which did nothing to promote the little girl's welfare?

First, an effective conciliation service for families on the point of disintegration may not have saved the marriage, but it may have helped both parents to take a less selfish and destructive attitude towards the sharing of the little girl after separation. In addition, it could well have picked up the fact that the girl was being given very little space to develop separately from her mother. At this stage it might have been possible to refer mother and daughter to a mental health clinic without this being interpreted as an attack on the mother's parenting ability. The clinic may have been able to help the mother to see that such a fusional relationship could in the long term cause serious harm to the child.

Secondly, although, once the case had reached court, the parties had become so firmly entrenched in their positions that any movement was virtually impossible and the hearing developed into a ritualistic slanging match over the issue of the sexual abuse, a sensitive judge might have been able to keep the child's interests in the foreground. This might have led to an order for supervised access to give the welfare officer service a chance to work with the parents towards reducing their hostility to one another and their use of the child as ammunition in their warfare. Ideally, the welfare officer service should be equipped to take on this kind of long-term work.

Thirdly, as for the child sexual abuse, it would be foolish not to acknowledge the possibility that the abuse, albeit of a minor nature, may have occurred. Supervision of the father's access should have acted as a deterrent for any future abuse and the supervision could have been reduced and ultimately dispensed with when the risk of abuse seemed negligible.

Case 3 (Chapter 2, p. 29)

This case concerned a young couple with housing and financial problems which, combined with lack of sleep caused by their children's sleeping difficulties and the stress of living in a confined space, led to fights between the parents and subsequently to physical abuse of the children. The court decision was for the children to be taken into care, where they were placed with foster parents. Some time later the parents lapsed into depression and drinking and visits to the children became infrequent and erratic. Despite the mother's desire to have the children returned to her, the view of the court was that she would be unable to cope on her own and the children were freed for adoption.

One aspect of this case which we did not reveal in the original discussion is that the maternal grandmother and other close relatives were living close to this family. Unfortunately, this grandmother resented her daughter choosing to marry a husband whom she disliked and therefore had very little contact with her grandchildren. However, subsequently, when the children had been taken into care and the marriage had disintegrated, she offered to help look after the children, but by then it was too late.

What could have been done?
First, when the problems between the couple emerged, much more could have been done to try to involve the extended family and get them to help with the care of the children. For example, the maternal grandmother might well have been able to offer some respite by looking after the children at weekends. Had this case occurred after October 1991 this outcome might well have been more likely, as the Children Act specifically draws attention to the need to look to the extended family as possible carers for children.

Secondly, when the children were removed from their parents, arrangements could well have been made for the grandmother and close relatives to have access to the children and to have them to stay some weekends. Once again the Children Act may have helped here.

Thirdly, after the disintegration of the marriage, and the mother's attempt to assume care of the children, it might well have been possible at that stage to involve members of the extended family. By concentrating narrowly on the nuclear family, the welfare professionals seemed to have overlooked entirely the possibility of retaining the children in the wider family network. Although hostility and lack of contact between extended family members may initially make it appear that the parents and children exist as an isolated unit, and also make it difficult for the parents to involve their relatives in their problems, the prospect that the children will be damaged or lost often leads to cooperation and solidarity between family members and to help and support for the children and parents.

Case 4 (Chapter 5, pp. 82–4)

In this case of sexual abuse a child aged four was referred by a High Court judge to the Clinic for assessment. The child had told her playgroup leader of various kinds of penetrative abuse she had experienced when visiting her father.

The girl's mother had suffered a deprived and disrupted childhood, having been brought up by a series of foster parents from the age of eight. She had married a man considerably older than herself and they had had one child. When the marriage broke down the father had continued to play an active part in looking after the girl. She used to spend long periods alone with him. For the mother this represented a relief from looking after her child who had become extremely difficult to handle, believing herself to be all-powerful and attempting to domineer and control every adult with whom she came into contact. She also wet and soiled herself and was aggressive towards other children. Her mother saw her in an entirely negative light. The child was driving her to despair, but at no time had she sought any help and none had been offered to her.

Once the sexual abuse had been alleged, the concern of social services and subsequently the court centred around this issue. Was there sufficient evidence or was it a figment of the child's fantasy? When the abuse could not be proved to the satisfaction of the judge, the court case simply fell apart. Mother and daughter were left to carry on their lives much as before with no additional help or support. The father had disappeared from the scene by this time, so access visits abruptly ceased. It was only six months later, when the little girl's behaviour became so bizarre that social services and the judge finally recognised that she needed urgent help, that a place was found for her in a residential home.

What could have been done?

Above all, this case provides a graphic illustration of the effects of myopic social policies towards child care which transform social workers into a sort of family police force whose primary task is to react to specific acts of abuse by protecting the child against the suspected adult. Long before she told the playgroup leader of the sexual abuse this child's behaviour must have exhibited tell-tale signs of disturbance which either passed unnoticed or were noticed but considered not a sufficient cause for intervention.

First, the sight of an isolated, single mother struggling to cope with an extremely difficult child should have alerted someone among the professionals with whom the family came into contact that all was not well. If the child had attended nursery school, instead of going to a playgroup for only two and a half hours a day for little more than half the weeks of the year, it may well have been that the family's problems would have been detected earlier and support offered.

Secondly, if someone had acted, mother and child could have been referred to a child mental health clinic. At that stage, work with mother and child would have stood some chance of success, whereas, as in the previous case, once court proceedings had been taken any chance of dealing with the problem in a non-combative way was effectively sabotaged. This work could have taken the form of a residential placement in a mother and child unit.

Thirdly, assuming that the sexual abuse had in fact occurred, the Clinic would have been well placed to address the issue in the context of therapeutic intervention rather than in the highly charged atmosphere generated by legal proceedings. It is much more likely that clear evidence of the abuse would have come out of this situation than from the narrow investigation that the Clinic was asked to conduct by the court.

Next, if the mother had rejected the need for any help for her child and continued to ignore the child's obvious problems, the matter could have been referred to an independent, informal hearing, along the lines that we discussed in Case 1. The object of this hearing would have been to obtain the mother's consent to and involvement in a programme of support for the child. If the mother still withheld her agreement, the panel or tribunal would have the power to implement such measures as were needed for the child's protection and the mother would have a right of appeal to a formal court.

Finally, since the father had disappeared from the scene by the time the court case was over, there was no question of access continuing. If he had remained, there would have been a major risk to the child in continuing her visits to her father, given the serious nature of the alleged abuse. Only if the father agreed to supervised access should he have been allowed to remain in contact with his daughter. Once again this could have been handled by an informal hearing with the possibility of the father applying to a formal court if he was aggrieved by the decision. It would probably have been to the little girl's long-term benefit to continue to see her father rather than all visits suddenly ending, but under no circumstances should she have been left alone with him in a situation where the alleged abuse could have recurred.

Discussion

We have set out our belief that the legal process, particularly where it takes the form of an adversarial contest fought out at an oral hearing, often proves to be incompatible with a child-centred approach to issues of abuse and family conflict. This belief is based on our experience of family cases which pass between court and clinic. The preceding chapters have concerned a detailed examination of the effects of legal intervention upon children, parents, social work practice and the therapy conducted by clinic staff.

Our re-examination of four of the case histories from earlier chapters reveals a further dimension to the protection of children and the management of child welfare which takes us back to the discussion of social policy issues in Chapter 2. The controversies which we have described over the most effective way to intervene to promote children's welfare are not merely local demarcation disputes between legal and clinical ways of doing things. They are also part of a much broader political debate concerning the alloca- tion and control of wealth and resources over a wide range of activities.

What we have experienced in recent years is the emergence of law as the dominant institution for the ordering of any intervention in relations between parents and children, and the extension, through Rules, Regulations and Guidelines, of legal concepts and procedures to cover every aspect of child welfare and protection.

This is not, as some legal commentators would have us believe, the inevitable consequence of the progress from disorder to order. They are rather the result of clear political choices. Once these choices have been made and child welfare issues start to become legal issues, *child law* comes to exist as part of the legal discourse, taking on a momentum of its own, generating a new brand of specialist lawyers, court social workers and guardians *ad litem*.

Specialised family courts and children's courts spring up creating new jobs, new vested interests to be sustained by a continual flow of legal cases. In England and Wales this process has culminated in the introduction of the Children Act 1989.

The collection of images that we have presented give some idea of the complexity of child welfare issues and of the enormous problems involved in understanding the way that families operate so as to identify how the child's best interests might be secured. They have also provided some evidence of the disruptive and destructive effects that the rigid and insensitive operation of legal process may have in practice. These images are a far cry from the simplified and idealised views of families, children and the legal and child welfare systems implicit in the Children Act and presented in the parliamentary debates, and in articles in legal and social work journals about the Act. Above all else is the assumption in the legal discourse that, once a child has been identified at risk of 'significant harm' or suffering as the result of hostility between its parents, people's behaviour will by and large become rational and sensible in their search for ways of meeting the child's needs. This assumption, however, is not borne out by the evidence that we have presented. On the contrary, when presented with highly emotive situations people, even lawyers and judges, tend to behave in irrational ways. Furthermore, the 'rationality' of child welfare may not, as we have seen, be the same as 'legal rationality' or 'economic rationality' when it comes to making decisions about children and their families. For reasons already explained, it is necessary for the law to maintain the myth of rationality even if it conflicts with people's actual experience of the way that families, social services departments, the police and the courts operate in practice, but the maintenance of the myth is not necessarily beneficial to children's interests.

The lesson for the future which we believe emerges from the evidence set out here is that, contrary to current beliefs in both legal and social work spheres, an effective child welfare or child protection policy does not depend primarily on the quality of the justice dispensed by the courts and legal system. Indeed, justice in the narrow legal sense may be counter-productive to the promotion of child welfare. Similarly, it does not depend upon the efficient and comprehensive codification of child care. Yet with the passing of the Children Act the point has been reached that, whenever a decision is required, social workers and mental health workers either have to consult lawyers or refer to an endless stream of Rules, Regulations, Guidelines and Directives designed to regulate their relations with children and their families. The sweeping juridification of a whole area of social activity which has taken place over the past ten or so years is reminiscent of the way in which law and the fear of legal repercussions had far-reaching effects on medical practice in the United States. The play-safe policies and decisions which such legal pressures provoke may in some cases benefit children. In other cases they may well have the opposite effect. Perhaps their most pernicious result, however, is that by transforming social problems into individualised legal problems, they mask the damage caused by lack of investment in those social areas essential for the healthy development of children – housing, education and health – lack of resources in the provision of substitute and relief care and lack of general preventive work with parents and children.

Principles for defining the limits of law

We end this chapter on a more positive note by setting out a series of principles which, like the principles of the Children Act referred to in Chapter 2, we would wish to see adopted by policy-makers. These are principles which in the first place restrict the negative impact of imposing legalistic interpretations and solutions on social and interpersonal problems, and, secondly, which provide clear and positive policy- and decision-making criteria.

1. Avoiding the dominance of legal 'truth'
As we have seen throughout the cases presented, the version of the historical truth set out in the legal decision may be rather different from that contained in a clinic's files or discussed at case conferences, because the assessment of people and past events are likely to have undergone very different selection and interpretation processes. These differences in processing serve the different objectives of courts and clinics and social work (see Table 7.1). For law, as we have illustrated, the objectives for which the establishment of truth is an essential element are concerned with managing conflict, conveying moral messages to the outside world about the way that adults should behave towards children and about the intrinsic fairness of the legal process itself and its ability to determine what is right for children.

The law's version of 'the truth' typically serves a process of coding the issues surrounding the child's welfare into a series of choices which the court is able or appears to be able to determine. This may take the form of a choice between two principles, for example, giving preference to the mother as opposed to not interfering with the children's present situation, where they are

Table 7.1 *Differences of process and objective between court and clinic*

Court	Clinic
Objectives	
Ensuring justice and equality between participants.	Defining children's needs.
Providing a stable, morally acceptable account of adult–child relationships.	Finding a solution which will provide security and stability for the child.
Promoting the legal process as capable of determining what is best for children.	Promoting the clinic as capable of determining what is best for children.
Procedures	
Formal rules designed to ensure fairness between the parties.	Ad hoc or semi-formal arrangements designed to investigate issues and define child's needs/problems.
Issues defined according to legal categories.	Issues defined according to professional areas of responsibility.
Preliminary process to reveal information and arguments in advance and encourage settlement.	Informal discussions with those involved in child's life.
Evidence	
Exclusionary rules to ensure admissible reliability of information, e.g. hearsay, previous convictions.	All relevant information.
Designation of experts – those permitted to give opinions.	All opinions admissible, but some given more weight than others.
Issues presented by oral evidence and tested for truthfulness by cross-examination. Once established, version of truth may be modified only by appeal.	Written or oral evidence accepted. Shared view emerges from combining information from different sources. Not definitive, the view may be modified as new information emerges.
After decision	
Matter returns to court only by demand of one of the parties.	Monitoring of plans to promote child's welfare. Plans adjusted according to results.

being cared for by their father and grandmother; or it may involve a choice between people or situations in identifying, for instance, which of the two parents is the *psychological parent*. Either way, the complexities and ambiguities, which characterise the clinic's versions of truth, are reduced to their simple proportions.

It is not sufficient, therefore, to explain away all the problems between court and clinic that we have recounted as mere misunderstandings, failures of communication or resulting from ignorance or prejudice on the part of the clinic or the judiciary. They arise, rather, wholly or in part from profound differences in the very nature of the different processes involved and the different objectives that those processes are serving. Table 7.1 contrasts some of these differences.

A major problem faced by both clinics and child welfare agencies at the present time arises directly from the need for the law to establish 'the facts' in order that legal determinations may be made upon those facts. The result is that much of the time and energy of social workers and clinical staff in England and Wales is devoted to investigative work to the obvious detriment of therapeutic and family support work. Furthermore, as we have demonstrated through several case illustrations, the role of investigator is largely incompatible with that of helper. In some cases the two roles conflict to such an extent that the chances of securing parental cooperation are totally jeopardised by the need to collect and present 'facts' in court.

Yet it does not have to be like this. Other countries have succeeded in separating the investigative role from the therapeutic role. In France, for example, investigations into child abuse are carried out mainly by prosecutors, court social workers (*éducation surveillée*) and by specialised sections of the police (*brigade des mineurs*), leaving social workers from social services and the voluntary sector free to work with the family. In Holland, confidential doctors, investigative social workers, lawyers of the Child Protection Council and the police are responsible for conducting enquiries into child abuse.

Some jurisdictions also succeed in avoiding the conflict of objectives arising from the dual role of courts to determine 'the facts' and assist in promoting the welfare of the child. In Scotland, for example, any disagreement by the parents or the child over allegations of child abuse are heard in the Sheriff's court, where disputed facts are subjected to a legal process of fact-finding. If proved, the matter is then transferred to the Children's Hearing where lawyers are rarely present. Most jurisdictions on the continent are sparing in their use of court hearings for fact-finding purposes. In Holland, the evidence presented to the juvenile court judge takes the form of a report from the Child Protection Council. Although lawyers may be present to represent children and parents, the facts set out in the report only rarely become an issue. (See also, the discussion of the French system in Chapter 8.)

2. Engaging the family

If one were to start from scratch and try to design an institution which was to concentrate exclusively on promoting children's needs, either directly or indirectly through education and persuasion of significant adults in the child's life, what would be likely to emerge would be very different from those family courts existing in most Anglo-Saxon legal systems. Perhaps the most important features that we would wish to see would be directed at involving rather than alienating the family.

This engagement of the family appears to us an essential element in any process which aims to respond to children's needs. Where the court's function is essentially that of resolving disputes, by the time the parties reach the courtroom door, they – whether they be the two parents or the social services department and the family – are likely to be very much at odds with one another. Engagement of the family, whether through cooperation between warring parents, or the willing involvement of parents who are resisting state intervention to protect their child, is often out of the question. Where it does occur, it takes place either at an informal level thanks to the efforts of conciliators or lawyers negotiating outside the courtroom or through the dogged efforts of individual judges who persuade the contestants to lay down their arms and try to work together in the interests of the children. Whether these attempts at engaging the family occur is a matter of chance rather than their being guaranteed by the legal system.

The Children Act, its Regulations and the Guidances published by the Department of Health on the operation of the Act, do go some way in the direction that we are proposing. These draw to the attention of social services departments the need to maintain family links by, for example, placing the child near the family home. Secondly, they require social services to consider the extended family as a potential resource for meeting the child's needs. However, the effectiveness of such exhortations in engaging the family will, as we have indicated, depend upon their taking place at an early stage, that is, before the legal process has polarised positions and made any cooperation extremely difficult. It will also depend upon there being resources available to allow, for example, children to be placed close to the family home.

The other set of requirements relates to joint planning between parents and local authorities for the child's future. The Children Act, according to the Health Department's Guidance 'assumes a high degree of co-operation between parents and local authorities in negotiating and agreeing what form of accommodation can be offered and the use to be made of it'. Parents, therefore, according to the Guidance, should be invited to attend reviews and should be consulted before any decisions are made concerning the child's future.

Admirable as such attempts to involve parents in the formal decision-making process may be, they need to be seen against a background of reinforcement through the law. Families and social services are not equal parties, so that any idea of partnership between them is to misrepresent the reality of the situation. The only power that aggrieved parents have is to invoke the law, and the Children Act with its codification of social welfare gives them ample opportunity to do so. Invoking the law in the English context, however, involves a move from cooperation to confrontation. If the case goes to court, it entails the making of a right/wrong decision, the creation of winners and losers and, so far as future prospects for cooperation are concerned, a much worse situation than existed previously. If the matter is settled through negotiation between the parties or their lawyers, the result will be a compromise between their respective interests and not necessarily the best solution from the child's point of view. We should add that the child is powerless in this negotiation process. The child has a right to be consulted as to his or her views, but that is all.

Such cooperation, reinforced by the threat of legal proceedings, is far removed from the notion of engaging the family that we would wish to see. To engage the family involves a process of understanding the family situation in all its complexity, and setting about the long and difficult process of changing the family dynamics through education and persuasion in ways which promote the child's interests and meet the child's needs. Often it will need the intervention of an independent authority figure to arbitrate where there is disagreement in ways that minimise the conflict and ensure that the child's needs are not forgotten in the quest for compromise.

3. Effective control over resources

A decision-making process which concentrates on children's needs presupposes that there are the resources available to meet those needs and that these resources are at the disposition of the decision-making body. It would be a rather pointless exercise if this were not the case. Say, for example, that it was decided that a child needed a daily period of nursery education in order to relieve the mother's stress, monitor the child's progress and improve his or her social skills. What would be the point of making such a decision if there were no places available in any of the state-run nursery schools and no funds which could be applied to pay for the child to attend a private school. Yet this is precisely the paradoxical position of the courts in relation to child welfare resources and services. Courts in most jurisdictions may shuffle the pack of parents, children and substitute carers by making orders as to who will live with whom and who will have contact with whom, but they cannot usually control resources. If there are no places in foster families, nurseries or children's homes close to where the child's family lives, the courts cannot create places. If financial stringencies have led to the social services' home-help facility being cut, the courts cannot decide on the provision of such assistance to a family where the mother cannot cope alone with the demands of child-rearing. The options open to the courts are determined, not by the law, but by the availability of services and resources for children and families.

The question then arises as to whether we would want the courts to be used to direct how and where child care resources should be deployed. Are court-driven social services departments, where resources are deployed according to what judges and magistrates identify as children's needs, really a good idea? Should not child care policy be decided by elected representatives in local and central government according to the broad needs of children and families as identified by professionals working in a particular geographical area? Many people find it repellent for decisions over hospital treatment to be made according to financial criteria rather than patient needs. Is it not equally unacceptable for child welfare decisions to be left to the lottery of the legal process?

This is not to question the appropriateness of any legal intervention where resource implications stem from the court's decision. Clearly, in some cases the quality and appropriateness of the substitute care offered by social services may be an important factor in the legal decision as to whether the child should remain in care or return to the family home. However, it does raise serious questions over the kind of situations that we described in Chapter 3 where legal proceedings were being used with the express intention of obtaining a court order to put pressure on the social services administration to find the resources necessary to help a particular child or family. Why should that child or family be favoured above others whose need may be as great, but whose problems are not amenable to legal proceedings? To allow judges in their judicial capacity to interfere with the policies of social services departments risks distorting those policies in ways that lead eventually to a court-driven child care system. For these reasons we would strongly oppose such a system, preferring the fight for adequate provision for children to take place in the political arena rather than in the courts. Decisions concerning resources to meet children's needs should be taken within the system that provides those resources.

4. *Promoting continuity in child welfare*

Throughout, we have drawn attention to the episodic way in which the law tends to intervene in the lives of children. This we have compared with the way in which institutions such as families, child welfare clinics and mental health clinics decide upon what is best for a child as a continuous process – a process which allows for adjustments whenever circumstances change and as the child develops.

Some countries have tried within the legal process to replicate this continual surveillance of the child's changing needs and fine-tuning in response to them. The French children's judges, for example, take upon their shoulders the personal responsibility (*suivi*) for the welfare of children who become the subject of a child protection *dossier*. Other countries, such as Holland, impose that responsibility only in a secondary capacity – the judge as super-supervisor. In both these cases the judge acts more in an administrative than in a judicial capacity.

In most Anglo-Saxon common law jurisdictions, law is kept separate and distinct from administration, so that matters generally come before the judge or magistrate for adjudication only where there is some dispute or where leave of the court is required to exercise some statutory power in relation to the child. An effective needs-related system of decision-making would clearly require continuity so that the people who make the decisions are ideally involved in the family, its problems, as they evolve and affect the child over a long period. Such continuity also enables decision-makers to act in a 'scientific' manner, their decisions reflecting the rapidly changing nature of childhood and the results of previous measures which have been tried in relation to the child and family. The law as it is practised in most Anglo-Saxon countries seems quite inappropriate for this kind of exercise. Rather it allows decisions to be made about children's welfare by people who see no more than snap-shots of the child's life.

So, to summarise, the basic requirements of a system designed to concentrate upon the needs of children are:
- The limited use of the legal system as the appropriate mechanism for determining issues concerning children's welfare.
- The capacity to engage the family in the child's future welfare.
- The ability to control resources or provide authoritative

directives to those controlling resources.
– Continuity in the involvement with the child and family.

Let us now in the final chapter take matters a stage further by discussing whether 'legal systems' can be made to incorporate these principles.

Further reading

The theory of law as an autopoietic system

Autopoietic Law: A New Approach to Law and Society edited by Gunther Teubner (De Gruyter, 1988).

How the Law Thinks about Children by Michael King and Christine Piper (Gower, 1990).

'Law as a Social System' by Niklas Luhmann, *Northwestern University Law Review* (1989) 83, nos 1 and 2, pp. 136–50.

Children's rights

Gillick v. West Norfolk and Wisbech Area Health Authority [1985] 2 Weekly Law Reports, p. 830, House of Lords.

The Rights and Wrongs of Children by Michael Freemen (Frances Pinter, 1983).

Proof and evidence in children's cases

The Evidence of Children: The Law and the Psychology by J.R. Spencer and Rhona Flin (Blackstone Press, 1990).

The Protection of Children by R. Dingwall, J. Eekelaar and T. Murray (Blackwell, 1983).

Report on the Evidence of Children and other Potentially Vulnerable Witnesses by the Scottish Law Commission (SLC no. 125, 1990).

The Report of the Pigot Committee Home Office (HMSO, 1989).

'There Is a Book Out . . .: An analysis of Judicial Absorption of Legislative Facts' by P. Davies, *Harvard Law Review* (1987) 100, pp. 1539–603.

Analyses of the Children Act 1989

Governing the Family. Child Care, Child Protection and the State by Nigel Parton (Macmillan 1991).

The Reform of Child Care Law: A Practical Guide to the Children Act 1989 by John Eekelaar and Robert Dingwall (Routledge, 1990).

8

What Kind of Decision-making System?

If, as we maintain, there are aspects of legal systems which are incompatible with the promotion of children's well-being, it is important for us to distinguish exactly what we mean by a 'legal system'. Throughout our discussion we have made one important distinction between law, meaning the legal system and process, and the judges, magistrates, lawyers and various court officers who are responsible for the system's operation. We now want to take matters a stage further and, in this final section, distinguish 'legal systems' from other decision-making systems. This distinction is not as obvious as it may appear. It is not enough simply to identify anything that occurs in courts or any decisions made by judges or magistrates as 'law', since in some jurisdictions, as we shall see, certain specialists operate in a way which has very little in common with the legal process. Conversely, calling a legal decision-making body 'a tribunal' or 'family council' rather than a court or appointing non-lawyers as decision-makers does not necessarily place the decision-making process outside the legal system.

A basic, if rather circular, definition of a legal system would be any decision-making body which produces legal decisions through the imposition of binary criteria of legal/illegal. What then are the features which characterise and distinguish these 'legal decisions' from other kinds of decision-making?

1. *The application of a binary legal/illegal code to a set of historical facts or intended future action.* This rules out bodies which decide how money should be spent or distributed, whether a person is healthy or unhealthy, whether a person has reached the standard required to pass an exam or be accepted into a professional body. All of these issues may become legal issues by being contested in the courts, but once this happens the criteria are those of the law and not those of the original decision-making body.

2. *The decisions are treated as law by other parts of the legal system.* This means, for instance, that they are capable of appeal through the normal legal channels. They are capable also of being reported in law reports and legal journals. On occasion, they may serve as precedents for other legal decisions. 'Legal decisions' are capable of being criticised or defended on the basis of their compliance or non-compliance with the law or procedural rules. The fact, for example, that an adoption ordered by a court results some years later in identity problems for the child does not make

it an illegal decision or a wrong decision in law. However, if the judge ignored certain procedural rights of the natural parents, then there could well be grounds for an appeal.

3. *The procedures by which the decisions were reached do not differ substantially from those in other areas of legal decision-making within the same legal system.* This does not mean to say that any deviation from a standard set of procedures means that the decision-making process can no longer be identified as legal. There may, for example, be more or less emphasis on written or oral evidence according to the rules governing particular kinds of cases. If, however, decisions are made as a result of round-table discussion, or a ballot of all those present, or if the decision-maker is known to have a strong personal interest in the result, then it is very unlikely that the decision can be identified as 'legal'.

4. *The decision-makers have been trained as lawyers or appointed or guided by people trained as lawyers.* Lay assessors who sit with a judge may therefore be involved in making decisions without removing the decision from the legal arena. Jurors who may decide cases in the absence of the trial judge but who are guided by him or her in how they should apply the law may also make legal decisions. A tax inspector, minister of state or surgeon, however, does not make legal decisions, although their decisions, once again, may become the subject of legal proceedings.

If all four of the above characteristics are present then it is clear that we are dealing with 'legal decisions' and the system which produces such decisions may be identified as a 'legal system'. English juvenile courts, American family courts, juvenile courts or children's courts are therefore legal systems. Conciliation programmes, New Zealand family councils, the Dutch Child Protection Council and Swedish Social Welfare Committees clearly are not. But what are we to make of hybrid systems such as the French children's judge or the Scottish Children's Panel?

The French children's judge

When acting in child protection, as opposed to delinquency cases, the children's judges (*juges des enfants*) in France hear all cases in their private offices (*cabinet*). There are no formal procedures. The judge is simply required to summon the parents, listen to them and do everything possible to secure their cooperation for any measure taken in respect of the child. Most hearings take the form of informal discussions between parents, social workers and, in the case of older children, the child, with the judge presiding. The judge may decide the order of the discussions and who will be present. There are no rules of evidence and no requirement that information which may influence the outcome should be presented at the hearing. Judges may, for example, talk on the telephone to the director of a children's home before the hearing and base their decision on what that director says about the child's progress. Lawyers may be present at the hearing but rarely attend, partly because there is no legal aid provision to pay for them and partly because their presence is unlikely to have much influence on the outcome.

When a child protection file is opened, the children's judge takes formal responsibility for that child's future welfare. Most orders are provisional and may be varied at any time, according to changes in the child's or care-taker's circumstances. Where a child is placed away from his/her parents, a provisional order is limited to six months, after which time the judge must make a definitive order fixing a time limit of not more than two years. This may be reviewed at any time either at the request of the child, parents or children's home or on the judge's own initiative. At the end of the two years or shorter period fixed by the judge, the judge must reconsider the child's situation.

So far nothing in the children's judge's jurisdiction has any of the essential features which we identified as characterising legal decision-making. Indeed, when compared to England, the judge's role would correspond more closely to that of the area manager of a social services department than that of a judge or magistrate. They have their own team of social workers (*éducation surveillée*) to assist them. They may allocate children to specific children's homes and may play a part in inspecting and approving finances for these homes and other social work agencies and therefore play a part in allocation of child care resources.

However, children's judges, while assisted by the *éducateurs*, are not themselves trained social workers. They are law graduates who have undergone two years' general training as career judges. After a period in the capacity of children's judge, many of them move on to other branches of the judiciary. Furthermore, the decisions of children's judges are treated as legal decisions in that they are capable of being appealed to the *Cour d'Appel*. It is significant, however, that where appeals succeed it is usually because the judge has failed to comply with the minimal procedural requirements, such as giving both the parents an opportunity to be heard. Even after a successful appeal, the case is usually returned by the *Cour d'Appel* to the children's judge since s(he) is seen as the only person who knows the family and child well enough to handle the case.

What one has in the French children's judge is a mixed or hybrid

system in which many of the features of legal systems that we identified as obstructive to the promotion of children's well-being have
been eliminated, while at the same time the status of the judge as
an impartial, authoritative arbiter has been retained, as has the
power (very rarely used) to enforce decisions coercively. It has to
be said that the system has been criticised both within and outside
France for the apparently unrestricted power that it places in the
hands of the judge. However, these criticisms tend to ignore the
informal pressures that exist to restrain individual judges from
taking decisions which are out of line with those of their fellow
judges in the *Tribunal pour enfants* or unacceptable to the team of
social workers, specialist police officers and prosecutors with
whom they work.

We should emphasise at this point that we are not dealing here
with the difference between inquisitorial and adversarial systems,
but that between systems designed to produce legal decisions and
those created to interpret and deal with child protection issues as
essentially family problems. It may well be that the inquisitorial
system existing in continental European countries facilitated the
creation of such a child and family-centred system, but there are
major differences between the inquisitorial system as it applies in
criminal and civil cases and the child protection jurisdiction of the
children's judge. We now go on to look at the attempt to construct
a family-centred decision-making process in a country where the
legal system is adversarial.

Scottish Children's Panel

The method which the Kilbrandon Committee and draftsmen of
the Social Work (Scotland) Act, 1968 devised for overcoming the
problem of child care cases turning into disputes over the facts and
the production of right/wrong decisions was to separate the legal
from the child welfare aspects of cases. This was achieved by
creating a decision-making body, the Children's Panel, that can
only take on those cases where both the child and parents accept
the facts or a previous court decision has established that the child
is at risk. Where the facts are disputed, the case is first referred to
a hearing in the Sheriff's court where all the trappings of legal
procedures are present, including legal representation for both
parents and child.

In practice, this separation is less than perfect, since all cases
involving children too young to agree the facts have to go before
the Sheriff's court, even though the parents accept the facts. None
the less, it does allow for the existence of a decision-making body

which, like the French children's judge system, succeeds in removing many of the elements which obstruct a problem-orientated, child and family-centred approach.

Panel members, the decision-makers of the Children's Panel, are not lawyers. Nor do they undergo training in law and legal procedures. Instead, they are members of the local community with a particular interest in children, and their training sessions concentrate on such matters as child development, family systems theory and communicating with children. Moreover, there is no legally qualified person present to guide them in their decisions. The Reporter, who plays an important role in the Scottish system investigating and selecting those cases to go before the hearing, presents the facts of each case and often offers guidance as to what solutions are available. Yet the Reporter has more usually been trained as a social worker than a lawyer.

At the hearing, Panel members, Reporter, social workers, parents and children usually sit around a table and discuss the situation informally. No lawyers are present to represent either the social services department or the family. Indeed, it is significant that the Children's Panel has successfully resisted demands for legal representation by arguing that it is not a court of law, but a hearing to decide what is best for the future welfare of the child. This distinction is all the more significant when one considers that most of the cases coming before the Panel concern children who have committed offences rather than child abuse or neglect cases.

As in the French system, the Children's Panel is linked to the legal system through the appeals system. Unlike the children's judges, however, the powers of the Scottish Panel members are strictly limited to the making of residential or non-residential supervision orders. Once the order has been made, all parental rights pass to social services. Yet, both the child care role and continuity of the Panel's involvement are maintained after the making of the order by annual reviews by the Panel and the requirement that any proposed changes in the child's residential arrangements go back to the Children's Panel Hearing.

We have not made any attempt here to give an exhaustive account of the French or Scottish systems, but have rather used them as illustrations of the scope for hybrid systems which overcome the sort of 'juridification' of child welfare and the domination by lawyers which we believe often have a negative impact on children and family problems. While these negative aspects are not confined to adversarial systems (witness, for example, the French divorce system), it is probably true to say that the inquisitorial system, with its emphasis on investigation and control by career judges and the continuous process of justice as opposed to the courtroom trial, leaves much more scope for hybrids, which escape the domination of law, to emerge within the court structure. In an adversarial system, such as exists in Scotland, the best way to avoid the reconstruction of child welfare issues as legal cases is to create a separate decision-making body outside the court structure. Until similar child welfare orientated hybrids exist in other adversarial jurisdictions, we see little chance of any significant change in the way that these legal systems deal with child care issues. For this reason we are not convinced that the major structural changes, the creation of new legal concepts and the massive training programmes resulting from the English Children Act 1989 will bring into existence the 'new deal' for children and families that is claimed by its supporters. Nor are we impressed by the frequent reforms and renaming of legal institutions that occur in American state jurisdictions. On both sides of the Atlantic the legal culture, and above all the jealously protected power and interests of the judiciary and the legal profession, are likely to present a major obstacle to the changes that we wish to see implemented.

In the area of private law, such as divorce and disputes between individuals over the care of children, the prospects are rather better. The conciliation movement – offering an alternative way of resolving disputes to that provided by the legal system – has already had a major impact in both the United States and Britain. However, even here there are problems in clarifying and institutionalising the relationship between conciliation decisions and the legal process in ways which do not result in conciliation sessions being brought within the legal system. The promotion by the British government of in-court as opposed to out-of-court conciliation, and in the United States the exploitation by lawyers of conciliation sessions to promote their clients' interests, are examples of these problems.

Our hope is that the evidence and arguments that we have presented here, and in particular the examples that we have given of the impact of the legal process on children and their families, will help to counter what we see as the powerful and prevailing rhetoric dominating much of the policy-making concerning child welfare issues. It is a rhetoric which presents the law, the imposition of legal duties and the granting of legal rights as capable of providing solutions not only to poverty and deprivation but also to complex social and psychological problems. These problems require for their solution time, sensitivity and, above all, a team of highly motivated, well-trained people working in adequately resourced institutions. The legal system may give the impression of being able to provide these, but in reality it cannot do so.

Further reading

The French system of children's judges

'Child Protection and the Search for Justice for Parents and Families in England and France' by Michael King, in *The Law, The State and the Family* edited by Michael Freeman (Tavistock, 1984).

The French Alternative: Delinquency Prevention and Child Protection in France by Peter Ely and Chris Stanley (NACRO, 1990).

'Judges and Experts in England and Wales and in France: Developing a Comparative Socio-legal Analysis' by Michael King and Antoine Garapon, *Journal of Law and Society* (1987) 14, no. 4, pp. 459–73.

The Scottish Children's Hearings system

'The Role of the "Children Hearings" in Child Abuse and Neglect' by F.M. Martin, K. Murray and H. Miller, *Child Abuse and Neglect* (1982) 6, pp. 313–20.

Social Work (Scotland) Act, 1968 (HMSO, 1968).

The Swedish system

'Children, Family and the State in Sweden' by David Bradley *Journal of Law and Society* (1990) 17, no. 4, pp. 427–44.

Intermediate decision-making structures

Taking Children Seriously – A Proposal for a Children's Rights Commissioner by Martin Rosenbaum and Peter Newell (Gilbenkian Foundation, 1991).

English juvenile courts

Magistrates at Work by Sheila Brown (Open University Press, 1991).

Index

lawyers *cont.*
  experts and the court experience
    91–107
  role in child care cases 100, 101–4
  tactics with experts 94–5
  training programmes for 104
  trustee role 103–4, 106
lay assessors 139
lay magistrates 10
learning theory 43
legal intervention
  dangers of 2–4
  effects of in sexual abuse cases 86–8
legal labels 82–4
'legal system', definition 138
local authority
  care proceedings 11
  and parents joint planning for
    child's future 133–4

magistrates 4, 9–10
magistrates' courts 9–10, 12, 13, 23
manic-depressive illness 48, 121–2
marital breakdown, and the court 18,
    55–67, *see also* divorce;
    separation, of parents
media publicity 1, 68
mediation 66, 117
mental illness, in parents 47–50
moral issues 68–9, 109
Morgan, Elizabeth 105
mothers, manipulation of children 58–9

National Health Service 22
needs, compared with rights 116,
  119–28
neglect 9, 25, 44–6
  cases of emotional 24
New Zealand, family councils 139
NSPCC (National Society for the
  Prevention of Cruelty to
  Children) 3, 11
nuclear family 20, 126
nursery education, scarcity of places 33

Official Solicitor 14, 55, 100–1

parent
  allegations of cruelty against the
    other 56–60

parent *cont.*
  the neglecting 44–6
  psychological 131
parental absence 56
parental responsibility 12, 15, 66, 113
parental rights, to challenge removal
  of children 113–14
parenthood, court and clinic
  perceptions of 35–54
parenting capacity, assessment of
  41–50
parents
  defensiveness of 51, 72–3
  intransigent 65–6
  and local authorities joint planning
    for child's future 133–4
  with mental illness 23, 47–50
  and 'reality' of the situation 99
  restrictions on use of wardship 13
  snap judgments and dilemma of
    50–2
patriarchy 22
persuasion, and coercion 111–12
Piggot Committee Report 111
place of safety order 8, 11
placement, close by family 133
play
  children's and behaviour during
    interview 80–2
  sexualized 69
police 9, 72
  in care proceedings 11
policy, ideology and resources 25–9
poverty 23, 25–7
prediction 43, 96
pregnancy, as a result of abuse 70
preschool children, symptoms of
  sexual abuse 69
preventive social work 30
primary school children, symptoms of
  sexual abuse 69–70
probation officers 12
procedural rights
  children's 116–17
  definition of 113
  parents' 113, 114
procedure, rules governing 16, 117
procedures, legal 139
'process-record' notes 39
promiscuity 70